# HORRIBLE SCIENCE

# WASTED WORLD

## NICK ARNOLD

illustrated by
## TONY DE SAULLES

D0040390

SCHOLASTIC

www.horrible-science.co.uk

www.nickarnold-website.com
www.tonydesaulles.co.uk

Consultant: Peter Littlewood,
Director, Young People's Trust for the Environment

Scholastic Children's Books,
Euston House, 24 Eversholt Street,
London, NW1 1DB, UK

A division of Scholastic Ltd
London ~ New York ~ Toronto ~ Sydney ~ Auckland
Mexico City ~ New Delhi ~ Hong Kong

First published in the UK by Scholastic Ltd, 2009

Text copyright © Nick Arnold, 2009
Illustrations © Tony De Saulles, 2009

ISBN 978 1407 10822 3

Printed in the UK by CPI Bookmarque, Croydon

4 6 8 10 9 7 5

The right of Nick Arnold and Tony De Saulles to be identified as the author and
illustrator of this work respectively has been asserted by them in accordance with
the Copyright, Designs and Patents Act, 1988.

# CONTENTS

**Nick Arnold** has been writing stories and books since he was a youngster, but never dreamt he'd find fame writing about the Wasted World. His research involved singing to iceburgs and making friends with a polar bear, and he enjoyed every minute of it.

When he's not delving into Horrible Science, he spends his spare time eating pizza, riding his bike and thinking up corny jokes (though not all at the same time).

**Tony De Saulles** picked up his crayons when he was still in nappies and has been doodling ever since. He takes Horrible Science very seriously and even agreed to sample radioactive sandwiches. Fortunately, he has made a full recovery.

When he's not out with his sketchpad, Tony likes to write poetry and play squash, though he hasn't written any poetry about squash yet.

# INTRODUCTION

Somewhere on the outer fringes of the Milky Way galaxy is a small blue planet that circles a rather average yellow star. Recognize this place? It's home, and unless you're an alien it's the only home you've ever known.

Actually, as planets go, the small blue planet is rather nice. There's tasty food to eat, and it's not too hot and not too cold (I'm talking about the weather, not the food). Oh yes, and the scenery isn't too bad either. No wonder every mad scientist in the universe wants to rule this world. See what I mean – here's one now!

ISN'T EARTH LOVELY? ALL THAT LOVELY GOLD AND MONEY! PITY I'M NOT RULING IT RIGHT NOW!

Nora Nasty — the Professor's mad assistant.

Clarence — an educated polar bear who has fallen into bad company.

EVIL SNIGGER!

IS THIS REALLY A GOOD IDEA?

Badog — a bad dog who sometimes shows signs of finer feelings.

THERE HE GOES AGAIN!

We'll catch up with the evil Professor and his gang later, but first I just wanted to say that there's something a bit odd about our planet. In fact, it's as odd as a store full of odd socks. We like living here, and it's the only home we've got, and yet we're trying to trash the place! And that's what this book is about.

In the next 138 pages you'll find out what's wrong with the Earth and check out our chances for the future. And because this book is called "Horrible Science" and not "Fairly Nice Science" you'll be getting all the stomach-turning squishy bits too. So what are we waiting for? The whole world is getting wasted and there's no time to waste!

# THE MIGHTY PLANET-MUNCHING MACHINE

Happy? Well, even if *you're* not grinning like a skeleton with a new bone, right now three-quarters of a million people are smiling. They're the proud parents of the 375,000 or so little humans born today. And that's lovely! We all like babies – trouble is, the ever-growing number of humans is putting a real strain on Planet Earth...

Right now these brand-new humans don't know anything about anything, but if they did they would probably be busy figuring out what they wanted from their new lives. They might even grab a crayon and scribble a shopping list...

My Shopping List By Baby Pipsqueak ──→

1) Now I've got a new life I want food. OK – so Mum's milk's fine for now – but I'm talking burgers and fries and crispy onion rings ... and soon! And I want feeding three times a day for the rest of my life or I'll SCREAM UNTIL I CHUCK!

2) And drink like slurpy shakes and cool cola. Every drink in the universe is based on water, so I guess I need clean water. And I might need to wash ... sometimes.

3) I want somewhere to live – ideally with my own bedroom, en-suite bathroom, TV and high-speed Internet connection.

4) I suppose I need an education. Well, my mum and dad reckon I do.

> **5** There's loads more that I want - like a lifetime's supply of luxury nappies and a wardrobe full of designer romper suits and a computer-controlled air-conditioned high-speed baby buggy with a built-in CD-player ... but just now I'm getting a bit sleepy.
>
> **6** Oh yes, and I need some sleep zzzzzzzzz

Get the idea? Every baby on the planet wants a share of the world's goodies – the trouble is there aren't enough to go round.

### DEADLY DATA-BURST

- By 2009 there were about 80 million more humans every year – that's roughly the population of Germany. And people were living longer, which meant that there were more people alive at the same time.
- Over 800 million people didn't get enough to eat and one billion didn't get any clean water.
- One in six people didn't even get a basic schooling, and what's more most of them wanted it.

Back in 10,000 BC human beings were almost as rare as a flying rhinoceros. Back then, there were only about ten million folks around to give woolly mammoths a bad-hair day. Just look at the graph below. In 1900 the population of the Earth was vastly greater, but still four times smaller than it was in the 2000s…

By 2030 there could be 8.2 billion of us and by 2150, 9.3 billion. And they'll all want food and water, shelter and education (whether they like it or not). And they'll all want to travel and they'll all want all the gadgets and toys that scientists can invent.

## Dare you discover ... how fast the population is growing?

*You will need:*
At least 64 sheets of paper*

*Note for optimists
If your parents are especially rich and gullible you could ask for 64 50-pence coins instead. You never know – you might get them. If so, tell your gullible parents that the experiment will last 32 years. Ideally the paper should be recycled – as you'll find out on page 119, recycled paper is kinder to trees and better for our planet.

*What you do:*
**1** Place two sheets of paper on a table. Each piece of paper stands for one person. Imagine these sheets are a couple of parents. They're not very healthy – I mean they're both as white a sheet, ha ha!
**2** Now place another two sheets of paper on top of the first two. You now have four sheets of paper (don't faint with amazement). Imagine these sheets are the first couple's four children. Add another four sheets and you'll get (well knock me down with a frozen budgie) eight grandchildren. Add another eight and you'll get 16 great-grandchildren.
**3** See what's happening? Every time you add sheets you make a new generation. And each generation is *twice* the

size of the previous one. So for the next generation you'll need to add another 16 sheets and 32 for the next.

**4** You can carry on adding sheets and doubling the numbers until you run out of patience, run out of paper or use up all the paper on the planet...

*You should find:*
The numbers soon add up. In fact you might be ever-so-slightly brain-boggled to read that after 100 doublings your paper pile would span the known universe and you would have to cut down all the trees in the cosmos to make paper. Clearly there won't be that many people on Earth or they might eat all the food and trample on each other's toes and lose their tempers and kill each other off.

And now for some good news... By 2070 the population won't be growing so fast. The reason for this is complicated, but the idea is that people are getting richer and having fewer kids to save money. Sounds odd? Well, rich parents spend more on their kids – so having loads of kids could be expensive. The trend towards smaller families has already happened in the USA, Europe and Japan.

Mind you, 9.3 billion is more than enough – I mean imagine cooking for that lot, and the washing up would be a nightmare. So how on Earth will the world cope? And will we make it to 2050? After all, one population expert reckoned we shouldn't be alive today...

## Hall of fame: Rev Thomas Robert Malthus
(1766–1834) Nationality: British

The first thing to know about Thomas Malthus is that he didn't call himself Thomas – he was Robert and don't you forget it. Tom, er, sorry I mean Rob, had seven brothers and sisters – so it's no wonder he was worried about exploding populations. If I had seven siblings I'd want to explode too. Mind you, Robert married his cousin Harriet in 1804 and they had three children of their own – so that was a 50 per cent increase in the population of his branch of the family.

Robert's dad was a philosopher who reckoned that everything would turn out fine. "Not necessarily," said miserable Malthus junior. "The problem is our food supply increases gradually depending on how much food farmers can grow."

But the population can double every generation. Robert reckoned that when the food supplies ran out, people would starve.

Robert became a priest and then a teacher, and in 1798 wrote a book on his ideas that became a bestseller. In fact his ideas were so influential that in 1834 a law in Britain ordered poor people to be locked up in workhouses. The idea was that you shouldn't help poor folk or they might have too many kids without increasing the food supply. So instead poor people were made to pull ropes apart with their bare hands and were fed on old bones and scraps.

Robert died in 1834. But even in death his tombstone continued to plug his book and drum up a bit of free publicity. Here's what the tombstone DIDN'T say…

**11**

✝ **R.I.P.** ✝

Here lies the body of Tom who was Rob
He was a teacher who was good at his job
And famous for his book on population
Which had a big impact on the rest of the nation
You can buy it still at a good bookstore
Even though Tom can't sign it any more
It says we shouldn't give the poor what they need
Because they'll only go off and breed
But at least now poor Tom's life is done
The population has dropped by one.

OK – so the tombstone didn't put it like that. What it did say was how famous the book was and what a good guy Tom, I mean Rob, was. And he was a good guy even though his book was used to justify unkindness to people in need and his ideas were all wrong.

Muddled Malthus got it wrong because in his day most work was done by human muscle power with a bit of help from our animal friends. And the wrong-headed reverend never imagined a world where machines made more of everything – with huge increases in the amount of food. Nor did he imagine giant container ships and planes to speed food from one side of the planet to the other, or freezers to keep it fresh, or electricity and oil to power everything.

You can imagine the whole world's industry and farming and transport as one giant machine – let's call it the "Mighty Planet-Munching Machine". This incredible contraption turns plants, animals and raw materials into paper and furniture and beefburgers and cornflakes and computers and cars and automatic nose-picking machines and everything you'd ever want for Christmas.

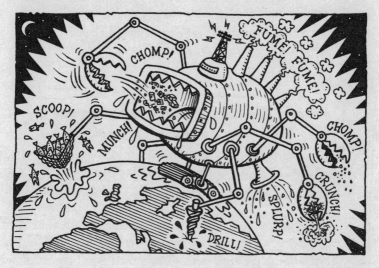

Now, there's no doubt that the Mighty Planet-Munching Machine is good at its job. It keeps most of us fed and it's made many people rich. But there's a price to pay – well, quite a few costs. Want a peek at the bill?

BILL FOR THE MIGHTY PLANET—MUNCHING MACHINE
For keeping you clothed and fed and sheltered and making whatever you want and taking you wherever you want...

COST – an endless supply of raw materials

The trouble is that Planet Earth is only 40,075 km around and there isn't an endless supply of anything, except maybe snot when you have a bad cold. And right now we're starting to run out of a few essential items...

## MISSING MINERALS

The Mighty Planet-Munching Machine needs ever-larger amounts of minerals to make more of what we want. By 2008 scientists were worrying that they were running out fast. The exact figures are open to argument but no one doubts that there's only so much of each substance in the ground and they won't last for ever. Welcome to the Horrible Science World Store.

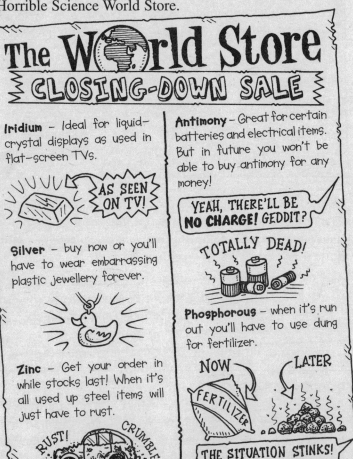

## The W🌐rld Store
### CLOSING-DOWN SALE

**Iridium** – Ideal for liquid-crystal displays as used in flat-screen TVs.

AS SEEN ON TV!

**Silver** – buy now or you'll have to wear embarrassing plastic jewellery forever.

**Zinc** – Get your order in while stocks last! When it's all used up steel items will just have to rust.

RUST! CRUMBLE!

**Antimony** – Great for certain batteries and electrical items. But in future you won't be able to buy antimony for any money!

YEAH, THERE'LL BE NO CHARGE! GEDDIT?

TOTALLY DEAD!

**Phosphorous** – when it's run out you'll have to use dung for fertilizer.

NOW    LATER

FERTILIZER

THE SITUATION STINKS!

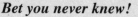

*Bet you never knew!*

*Platinum is used to make catalytic converters in cars. These devices cut down on pollution but platinum is scarce and expensive. So desperate boffins are trying to salvage platinum from roadside dust using microbes. The dust contains traces of platinum coughed out by car exhausts. By the way, lying in roads collecting dust samples isn't going to make you rich, although you might collect some interesting tyre marks on your body.*

But some things from the ground are going even faster than the minerals. I'm talking about the fuels we use to power the Mighty Planet-Munching Machine. According to scientists we've got…

• About 203 cubic km of oil left.
• About 192,000 cubic km of gas.
• Less than 847 billion tonnes of coal.

These may sound huge amounts but we could be running out of oil by 2060, gas by 2080 and coal around 2160.

These fuels are called "fossil fuels" because they're the preserved remains of things that were once living and they take millions of years to form. That means that when the fuels have gone there won't be any more for a few million years. But it's not just minerals and fuels that we're guzzling like there's no tomorrow. We're also destroying rainforests quicker than they can recover.

## RUINED RAINFORESTS

Rainforests are a biologist's dream. Of all the millions of types of plant and animal on the planet, about half live in rainforests. The plants include many vital medicines used by doctors, and the ingredients of about 80 per cent of the food you enjoy. Let's imagine you're slurping a giant-sized vanilla-and-pineapple-flavour ice-cream sundae with a choccie bar stuck in the top. Well, that delicious vanilla, pineapple and chocolate all came from rainforests.

So we ought to be looking after rainforests – right? Well, yes we *ought* to be!

### DEADLY DATA-BURST

• Figures vary, but rainforests could be shrinking by an area as big as five football pitches every second.

• In the first five years of the 21st century the Amazon rainforest in Brazil lost an area the size of Greece. Can you imagine losing Greece?

• Most experts agree that if people continue cutting down rainforests at this rate there won't be too much left by 2050.

As more and more rainforest is lost, the plants and animals can't breed or find new places to live. Many creatures have been wiped out before scientists even had a chance to study them…

*Bet you never knew!*
*One such bumped-off beast was a rainforest frog from Australia. This fascinating frog swallowed its own eggs and let the tadpoles swim around in its stomach juices. Then it puked up the babies to give birth.*

BLEURRRRRGH! YOU KIDS MAKE ME SICK!

But why the rainforest wrecking – don't we like frogs? Well, the problem is that rainforests are too useful for their own good. They're full of things that the world's booming population can't get enough of. I'm talking about…

**Trees** People want more and more lovely rainforest hardwoods such as teak and mahogany. It's a shame that the people cutting down the trees often don't bother to plant new ones.

**Land** People cut down trees to grow crops or raise cattle. So it's a pity that the soil needs trees to protect it from being washed away by rain. (They're not called rainforests for nothing.) In a few years you end up with a flooded wasteland.

**Minerals** Mining in rainforests means more roads and more trees cut down.

**Meat** In parts of Africa the only meat that people can afford comes from rainforests. Obviously we're not talking ham and bacon – we're talking crocodile and hippo and monkey-burgers. The trouble is, these animals are being bumped off faster than they can breed. Personally I think you might need a strong stomach to sample one. Monkeys often have their heads and hands cut off and their bodies smoked to stop them rotting. This isn't very nice, so let's talk about fish instead…

## EMPTY OCEANS

The Mighty Planet-Munching Machine isn't just wrecking rainforests – it's emptying the seas too. In all the time since the downfall of the dinosaurs there has never been a worse moment to be a fish. In the past, fishing boats were small and slow, and some of our finny friends could escape – but these days huge factory ships grab everything in the sea. As a result we catch four times more fish than we did in the 1970s. The bad news is that there aren't four times more fish in the sea.

Right now, scientist and inventor Professor N Large is shopping for some essential supplies for his cat, Tiddles…

18

The Prof shouldn't be too upset – there are plenty more fish in the sea. Er, no there aren't. And along with fish, those nasty nets haul in thousands of unlucky seabirds and dolphins. We talked to Baiji the world's unluckiest dolphin…

## The Horrible Science interview
with Randall Scandal

**RS:** So why are you so unlucky, Baiji?

**B:** Well, I'm dead…

**RS:** Oh dear – that does sound unlucky! How did you come to be deceased?

**B:** For thousands of years me and my dolphin chums lived in the Yangtze River in China. We baijis were a unique type of dolphin that couldn't see too well in the murky water – but we were happy.

**RS:** So you were smirking in the murk?

**B:** We were until the 1950s, when you humans started hunting us to make into handbags and gloves. And you caught us in your fishing nets.

**RS:** I guess you were fuming?

**B:** No, the river was fuming. We had to put up with your pollution too! We were cross until you wiped us out – then we were dead cross.

**RS:** That must have been "no fin".

**B:** My life had no porpoise.

**RS:** Are you still cross with us?

**B:** I'd take a bite out of you, but I'm feeling a bit stuffed.

**RS:** That's because you are stuffed.

**B:** Grrrr!

BAIJI IN HIS LOVELY NEW HOME

In 1980 there were about 400 baijis. By 1985 this figure had halved and by 1998 there were just 13 left alive. In 2006 scientists cruised 1,669 km of the river looking for the dolphins. Then they did it again. They found nothing at all.

Mind you, we're not talking about a few finished-off fish and the odd died-off dolphin – I could have mentioned any number of bumped-off beasts. But the misdeeds of the Mighty Planet-Munching Machine go way beyond these trifles. In fact, the whole of the rest of this book is about the damage – but let's start with some smelly dangerous stuff...

SOME THINGS TO LOOK FORWARD TO IN THE NEXT CHAPTER.

DANGER TOXIC!!

# TROUBLESOME TRASH

This chapter is a load of rubbish. I mean it's all about waste – gruesome garbage, putrid pollution and toxic trash. So let's talk rubbish…

### THREE THROWAWAY RUBBISH DEFINITIONS

*Garbage* = stuff we don't need and don't want. (Kindly note – these are *things* and not people such as little brothers/sisters. It's very unkind to stuff unwanted family members in dustbins.)

*Toxic waste* = garbage harmful to people or other living things.

*Pollution* = any garbage or toxic waste that escapes into the air, seas, soil or rivers.

### TEN-SECOND TOXIC TEST

Can you sort out the following into garbage or toxic waste?

**1** DOGGY POO

**2** UNWANTED SCHOOL DINNER

**3** INSECT KILLER

**4** ANTIFREEZE

**5** WASTE BATTERIES

**6** USED BANDAGES COVERED IN CRUSTY DRIED BLOOD AND PUS

**7** RADIOACTIVE SANDWICHES

Sorting through a pile of rotting garbage isn't everyone's idea of fun but it happens that hungry polar bears often look for food on rubbish dumps. It also happens that Professor Z accidentally threw out his evil plan for world domination. So he's ordered Clarence and Badog to find it…

## PROFESSOR Z'S EVIL PLOT THE RULE THE WORLD

Any old polar bear can see that we're the most wasteful life forms in the galaxy. Fancy a quick data-burst?

### DEADLY DATA-BURST

• Along with all that food and packaging, every year Americans dump 85 million tonnes of paper and cardboard. About half of this comes from newspapers and magazines. At the same time the world throws out over 360 million tonnes of paper and cardboard made from over four billion mashed-up trees.

- The average US family uses 500 glass containers. Although glass can be recycled, much of it ends up in the bin. The rest of world is just as greedy for glass – for example, the British use about 2 million tonnes of the see-through stuff.

- In the same year, each American dumps 125 kg of dead plants making a total 30 million tonnes of cut grass, not to mention the odd banana skin.

- People have invented 50 types of plastic but haven't worked out how to recycle most of them.

Maybe we're stupid. After all, some people think that when they chuck something away – an inflatable parrot or a screwed-up school report, it vanishes by magic. It doesn't. It gets dumped somewhere. Take plastic bags for example. Plastic bags aren't just embarrassing to be seen with – they're bad for the planet. We caught one trying to escape down the street on a windy day and put it on trial for crimes against nature. All rise for the Judge!

# The Horrible Science Trial

**Judge:** You, plastic bag of no fixed abode, are charged with the following crime: Every year billions of you get thrown away, but you take over 100 years to rot. How do you plead?

**Bag:** Not guilty – I'm a hold-all not a know-all! I can't help the way I was made. Anyway, who made me? Who threw me away? It was you humans! Mind you – I can handle myself, geddit?

**Judge:** When you get into the sea you look like a jellyfish and choke sea turtles and dolphins when they try to eat you.

**Bag:** You must be choking! It's not my fault is it? I mean, they're the ones who are trying to eat me! And so what? You humans still need me to carry your shopping.

**Judge:** That's where you're wrong! Whenever people have to pay for plastic bags they always end up bringing their own reusable bags.

**Bag:** So am I free to go?

**Judge:** No – you'll be five pence from now on.

Plastic bags are bad – but toxic waste is worse. I'm very sorry to say that someone's dumped a load of terrible toxic trash on the next page…

### PROFESSOR Z'S EVIL PLOT THE RULE THE WORLD

The story so far… The Professor has found his evil plans for world domination on the rubbish dump. For the first part of his evil scheme he's sent Clarence and Badog to collect toxic waste.

**1** Dioxins – come in 75 varieties. Evil effects include disrupting hormones – chemical messengers in your blood that help your body function. They also cause breathing problems and cancer.

**2** Radioactive waste – some atoms fall to bits producing harmful and invisible rays. Radioactive waste contains these atoms. The most dangerous of these is plutonium-239 – deadly for hundreds of thousands of years.

**3** Organochlorines – found in batteries and paint. Causes sickness, diarrhoea and headaches.

**4** PCB (that's polychlorinated biphenyls if you really want to know). Before they were banned they were used in electrical equipment. They cause cancer and damage the body's ability to fight disease.

**5** Oil refinery sludge – contains lots of poisons including hydrogen sulphide that smells of rotting eggs.

**6** Mercury – causes madness, loss of teeth and brain damage.

**7** Pesticides – killer chemicals designed to bump off weeds and unwanted insects, but they also bump off humans in large doses. Some pesticides have been linked to cancer and brain damage.

MUCH LATER

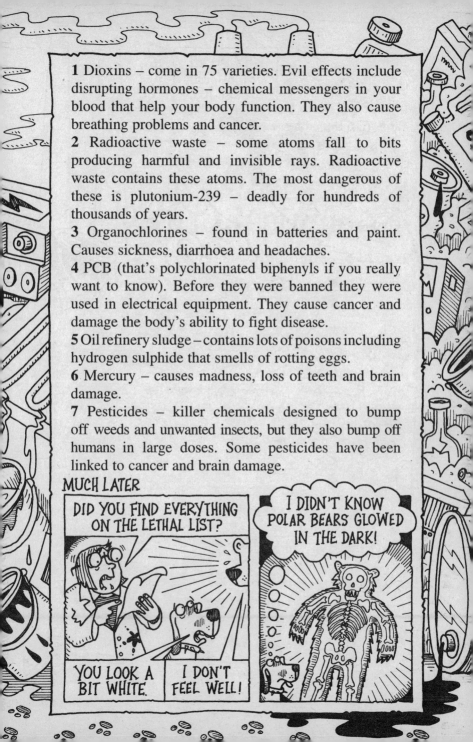

Even though it's against the law, some richer countries have been dumping their nasty waste on poorer nations. In 1988 the *Karin B* sailed from Italy to Africa to fetch a cargo of dumped toxic waste. Fancy a cruise?

Horrible Holidays present...

# Enjoy a Chemical Cruise!

Sail from romantic Italy to exotic Africa and back again!

DON'T RUSH BACK!

COUGH! SPLUTTER!

▶ Get away from the crowds (most people will get away from you).

▶ Meet lots of friendly locals (yes, all that shouting and waving banners is just their way of making you feel welcome!).

▶ Cruise Europe from Spain to Wales – but don't expect to land. Free souvenir drum of toxic waste. Your friends will be green with envy – in fact they'll be almost as green as you are!

The *Karin B* tried to land her deadly cargo in five countries. But no one wanted her lovely poisons and so she sailed back to Italy. Mind you, it's no surprise that people don't welcome toxic waste with open arms. When toxic trash gets in the wrong place the results are worse than terrible – they can be tragic…

## THREE TOXIC TRAGEDIES

**1** In the 1950s and 1960s people in Haginoshima, Japan, flooded their rice fields with water from a local river. But they didn't know that the river was polluted with cadmium – a heavy metal. Cadmium has a long list of nasty effects on the body, including fever, muscle pain, liver damage and softening of the skeleton. Just standing up can break your bones. By 1968, 100 people had died.

**2** Would you like to live in Love Canal? It sounds romantic and it's close to the lovely Niagara Falls. Pity they built it in the 1950s on top of a toxic-waste dump. When people started developing cancer and breathing problems, the whole town had to be closed down.

**3** Hopefully they didn't move to Times Beach, Missouri. In 1971 someone had the idea of spraying waste oil on the dirt roads. Trouble was, the waste contained deadly dioxins. In 1983 the toxic town had to be moved.

These dreadful disasters were bad enough – but what happened at Bhopal, India, was far, far worse…

## DEATH IN THE DARK

*Bhopal, India, 3 December 1984*

By midnight the poison had been boiling out for 90 minutes and a huge feather-like plume of white vapour was hissing up the useless flare-tower of the giant chemical factory. Heavier than air, the vapour sank and swirled in the blowy night and spread out in a low, deadly creeping cloud. But no one noticed. Bhopal slept under the bright stars in a haze of smoke from cooking fires and braziers. Few people were awake in the narrow streets around the factory.

It was 12.30 and the alarm still hadn't gone off. It had been switched off for fear of upsetting people. Soon they would be dead.

The deadly cloud contained methyl isocyanate (MIC) – a pesticide ingredient. Water makes MIC boil and somehow water had found its way into the MIC tank. When the MIC boiled, a faulty valve gave way.

There had been danger in the air of Bhopal for years – it was an accident was waiting to happen. Valves leaked, pipes corroded and the flare-tower would have blown up if it hadn't been disconnected. In 1982 a brave reporter named Rajkumar Kerwari had written a series of articles pleading for greater safety…

## BHOPAL IS SITTING ON A VOLCANO!
It is a warning for all the people

…and if you don't understand this you will be wiped out.

The people in power hadn't listened and now it was too late. That night every safety procedure failed.

Urged on by the chilly wind, wraiths of poisonous gas stole through alleys amongst the ramshackle houses and crept under doors and through broken windows. People woke in the dark with their eyes and noses and throats burning. When Asiza Sultan woke up all she could see was the white cloud, and people were shouting: "Run! Run!"

Then she started to cough and choke. Every breath felt like fire. Her eyes were burning. She ran. Everyone was running and sirens were blaring through a fog of death. The whole town was running – but none of them knew where they were heading.

Champa Devi Shukla ran with her family. She had never felt such pain. She felt as if her body was burning with red-hot chillis. Through eyes blurred with burning tears she glimpsed people falling around her. Their spit and snot was boiling and frothing, and their skin turned blue as their lungs collapsed. People were trampled in the rush to escape and cows tore through the streets bellowing in pain. There was no time to help anyone.

Hundreds of choking people made for the hospital but when desperate doctors rang the chemical company pleading for help they were told to bathe the victim's eyes in water. There were no medicines and no plan. To this day no one knows how many people died, but in the morning the streets were full of bodies – dead cows and birds and humans. Hundreds more were thrown in the river or dumped in the forest. But there were thousands of survivors too – lucky to be alive. And none of them would forget the night when death came in the dark.

## EXTREME INCINERATORS

One way to get rid of toxic waste is to burn it in a giant furnace called an incinerator. I've heard there's something about incinerators in Professor Z's new children's book – let's take a look. Hmm… I'm not sure I agree with all of this, but it does tell you how an incinerator works.

# EVIL SCIENCE PROJECTS FOR BOYS AND GIRLS

## HOW TO TURN YOUR SCHOOL INTO A TOXIC WASTE INCINERATOR

Most school buildings are completely useless, so I'm sure no one will mind if you use yours to make a few million dollars!

Instructions:

1 Clear everyone out of the school (and that includes the teachers). I expect once they see your toxic waste they won't hang about, ha ha!

2 You'll need to alter your school a bit. Start by converting the school boiler into a giant furnace that burns at 1,300°C, with a 40-metre-high chimney to let the hot gases escape.

3 Don't forget to install conveyer belts in the school corridors to take the waste to the incinerator. You'll also need special equipment to remove acid gases and toxic dust from the smoke.

4 Borrow your teacher's fan to waft the hot gases up the chimney. Incinerators use bigger fans for this job.

5 You could fire up your furnace using unwanted paper such as homework and school reports.

6 You can use the heat to boil water to make steam that can power generators and make electricity – or maybe use it to boil your enemies alive in a big vat of oil. You can sell the electricity to your friends and use the money for evil projects – it's not cheap being an evil genius, let me tell you!

WE NEED MORE HOMEWORK...

EH?!

TO FIRE UP THE FURNACE!

Scientists are working on other treatments that don't involve burning tonnes of toxic trash in your school. For example, certain trees and plants, such as alpine pennycress, are great at taking up toxic waste from polluted soil. The poisons stop hungry plant-eaters from lunching on its leaves

OOH, I DO LIKE A BIT OF CONTAMINATION...

HMMM, WE DON'T WANT YUMMY TOXINS GOING TO WASTE!

SLURP! SUCK! SLURP! SUCK! YUCK!

***Bet you never knew!***
*US scientists have discovered how make lemon oil from old tyres. They turn the tired tyres into gas at 725°C and the isoprimer molecules (molecule = a clump of atoms) form lovely lemon oil. You can put it on your pancakes if you don't mind getting a lemon-flavoured flat tyre.*

Talking about energy, that Mighty Planet-Munching Machine has yet another nasty surprise up its sleeve. But I'm not going to spoil your day by telling you now. I'll spoil it in the next chapter instead...

IT SMELLS BAD ENOUGH...

# EVIL ENERGY

Every machine – from your dad's car to an automatic wobbling toilet seat – has one thing in common. I don't mean that it breaks as soon as the maker's guarantee has run out. I mean it needs to get ENERGY from FUEL. And it doesn't matter if the fuel is dried camel dung or kryptonite crystals – without power, the machine is as useful as a teacher who has lost his voice.

Fuel and energy are easy to get your head round. We asked Professor N Large to explain them to the stupidest boy in the known cosmos – Sam Watkins…

### THE IDIOT'S GUIDE TO FUEL
With Professor N Large and Sam

*Sam:* What's fuel?
*Prof:* Fuel is anything that stores energy. It could be petrol or food…
*Sam:* Is that why I'm *fuel* up after a big meal?
*Prof:* Ha ha – very funny.
*Sam:* So what's energy – is it what I don't have in the morning?
*Prof:* Energy is the ability to do work.
*Sam:* My teacher says I haven't got the ability to do wxork.
*Prof:* For scientists like me – the word "work" means any kind of movement. It could mean heating something up.
*Sam:* So when I stay in bed I'm using no energy and doing no work?
*Prof:* Correct.

*Sam:* My dad says we ought to be saving energy. Can I save energy by not going to school?

*Prof:* Er…

*Sam:* And can I have a choccie bar? I feel a fuel crisis coming on…

*Prof:* Will you shut up!

The Mighty Planet-Munching Machine gets its energy from fuel in the form of wood, coal, oil and gas. Burning fuels produce heat (please don't gasp too loud – your teeth might fall out) and heat powers turbines to make electricity or machines that do work.

So are you a high-energy scientist? Have you got a power-fuel brain or are you just a little fuelish?

### HIGH ENERGY QUIZ

Simply match up the fuels to their sources. Warning – one possible answer is as useless as the virus that caught a cold…

**Fuels:**

1 Wood

2 Gas

3 Oil

4 Coal

**Possible answers:**

**a)** Cow guts.

**b)** Rotting bodies of tiny sea creatures that died in the time of the dinosaurs.

**c)** Dead fish – if you can catch any.

**d)** The squashed remains of giant plants called horsetails from 300 million years ago. (That's older than the dinosaurs and even older than your fossilized teacher.)

**e)** Trees.

35

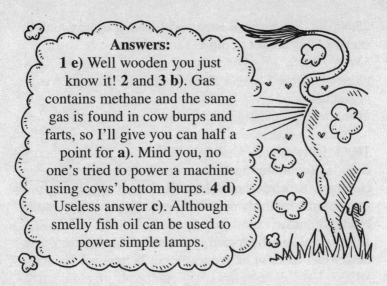

**Answers:**
**1 e)** Well wooden you just know it! **2** and **3 b)**. Gas contains methane and the same gas is found in cow burps and farts, so I'll give you can half a point for **a)**. Mind you, no one's tried to power a machine using cows' bottom burps. **4 d)** Useless answer **c)**. Although smelly fish oil can be used to power simple lamps.

And now it's time for a burning issue. Whenever you set fire to anything – a tank of petrol or an unwanted school report – you create pollution. And pollution contains unhealthy substances. That's why it's not clever to breathe in smoke – either from cigarettes, car exhausts or your neighbour's dried camel-dung bonfire. Humans have been setting fire to things for a long time – here's a quick time-tour. (You may want to hold your breath.)

## THE SMOKY SMELLY STINKING STORY OF BURNING POLLUTION

**1 million BC** Ancient ancestors of humans start using fires to cook with. Twenty minutes later they burn their supper and invent rude words.

**20,000 BC** People in Russia and Poland burn mammoth skeletons – I bet they enjoyed a good bone-fire.

**1306** Fumes from workshops bother English King Edward I – in fact they really get up his royal nose. He tries to ban the stink but no one takes any notice.

I'VE WORKED MY WAY TO THE TOP!

**1600s** People are burning more coal, and children get sent up chimneys to keep them clean. It was a brush with danger for the cowering kids.

**1800s** Coal powers steam engines that power factories. Children have to work the machines 12 hours a day.

**1859** Edward Drake drills for oil in Pennsylvania, USA. He uses the oil to make kerosene for lamps. Nowadays kerosene powers jet engines – that's progress for you!

**1879–1880** London is so polluted that there is four months of smoky fog. This is later known as "smog" – can you guess why?

**1952** London gasps in thick yellow smog. Hundreds of people die in road accidents. Smog mingles with moisture to make acid chemicals that attack the lungs. Thousands of people die of lung diseases.

**1970s** Los Angeles is covered in smog caused by the effect of sunlight on petrol and car exhaust fumes.

**2008** Polluted air kills millions of people every year.

OK – you can breathe easy now – but only for a minute. Then we're off to the most polluted spot on our very smelly planet...

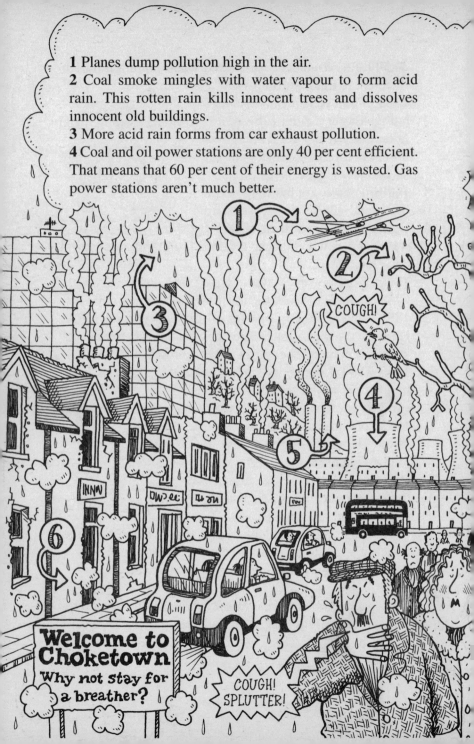

1 Planes dump pollution high in the air.
2 Coal smoke mingles with water vapour to form acid rain. This rotten rain kills innocent trees and dissolves innocent old buildings.
3 More acid rain forms from car exhaust pollution.
4 Coal and oil power stations are only 40 per cent efficient. That means that 60 per cent of their energy is wasted. Gas power stations aren't much better.

**5** Oil refineries can cause air and water pollution by 100 different harmful substances.

**6** Car exhausts blast out tiny bits of matter called particles. The perilous particles are linked to human deaths from heart disease and breathing problems.

**7** Whenever fuel is burnt in power stations, car engines or industry you get carbon dioxide – but I'll tell you about this gruesome gas in the next chapter.

## COULD YOU BE A SCIENTIST?

US scientists in Los Angeles have tested the effects of car exhaust particles by parking a trailer near a busy road for a few weeks. But who did they get to breathe the smelly dangerous fumes?

**a)** Other scientists
**b)** Their children
**c)** Mice

WHEEZE!

### Answer:

**c)** It was the medium-sized particles that did the damage since they travelled deeper into the lungs and stayed there longer.

## SO FAR - SO BAD. BUT GUESS WHAT?

This chapter is about to sink from dismally down in the dumps to stuck at the bottom of a coal mine. You might think that since pollution has putrid effects and fuels are running out, industry bosses and governments might be trying to use a bit less. Well, you might think that because you're sensible – but in fact we're using *more* fuel than ever!

The reckless, relentless, ruinous reason is that the whole world has become deeply dependent on fuels – especially oil. To prove it we're visiting the bathroom of top TV naturalist Will D Beest – seen here with his rather more intelligent pet monkey, Mickey…

## WILL D BEEST IN … IT'S A WASH-OUT!

Let's imagine Will's bathroom in a world without oil…

**1** No shower curtain – it's plastic.

**2** No shampoo, deodorant or shower gel because oil is needed to make plastic bottles. There's no doubt – life is drastic without plastic.

**3** No paint – it's oil-based.

**4** No heating or lighting because no oil-fired power stations.

**5** No toilet roll – the paper can't be made without energy and if lorries have no fuel nothing can be distributed.

**6** No plastic bath or shower.

**7** And no plastic duck either.

41

42

**1** Between 1990 and 2004 plane travel increased 120 per cent and it looked set to treble by 2030.

**2** The world guzzles four billion tonnes of oil per year.

**3** Each year the world buys more and more electrical gadgets – everything from computers to digital earwax removers – and they all need power, which means more power stations.

**4** And the world is buying more cars. In the 1960s there were 70 million cars in the USA. By 2008 there were over 200 million. In the US each driver travels an average of 65 km every day. If just one person did the driving they would have to cover 17.5 billion km every day. I bet they'd be bursting for the loo.

**5** Homes are bigger and warmer than they ever used to be – so they need more power.

**6** Fewer people choose to walk or cycle because the streets are too noisy and dirty and smelly and dangerous.

By 2008 the world had over 5,000 big polluting power stations and 3,000 big polluting industrial sites – with more on the way. But the energy-hungry, coal-chomping, wood-chewing, oil-swilling Mighty Planet-Munching Machine was doing something worse than making foul stinks. It was changing the weather too. There's something in the air and it's not very nice…

# CRAZY CLIMATE

The story so far – the greedy Mighty Planet-Munching Machine (otherwise known as all the world's farming, transport and industry) is busy gobbling minerals and fuel, and turning them into pollution and rubbish and toxic waste. And even though the world's fuel is running out there's plenty left to give our planet a bad case of the hots...

## FIRST A FEW USEFUL WORDS...

*Weather* = the amount of sun, rain, snow, cloud or fog you get each day.

*Climate* = the average weather you can expect from year to year.

*Atmosphere* = the layer of air around our planet including the dreaded greenhouse gases (see below). You might think the sky is big but the atmosphere isn't too thick. If you drove a car straight up in the air you'd be in space in ten minutes. If Earth was the size of a beach ball the atmosphere would only be as thick as a layer of paint.

*The greenhouse effect* = the result of certain gases heating the atmosphere, and nothing to do with growing the biggest pumpkin in the village.

*Global warming* – the effect of heating the atmosphere, and nothing to do with being told off for scoffing your supper too fast. That's a gobble warning.

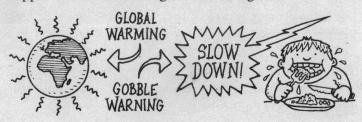

## TEACHER'S TEA-BREAK TEASER

Drum your fingers lightly on the veneer of the staffroom door. When your teacher opens the door, dazzle her with your sunny smile and politely enquire…

**Answer:** There's a 0.0000000001 per cent chance that your teacher will send your class home early – but to be honest it's not terribly likely. Nevertheless, it's true that global warming does shorten the days by speeding up the Earth's spin. As the oceans warm, water heads towards the poles, making the planet thinner around the middle. This cuts the day by 2.3 thousandths of a second every 100 years. Your teacher won't know this – or that global warming speeds westerly winds and this makes the day *longer* by one thousandth of a second. And if you happen to be a maths genius you'll have already worked out that the day will only be 1.3 thousandths of a second longer and that's not worth getting excited about unless you happen to be an extremely boring scientist.

But we're not like that! In fact we're so not boring that we're going to take our lives in both hands and meet the gruesome global greenhouse-gas gangs…

# The Greenhouse-Gas Gangs

by Chief Inspector Gas-Bag

Description of vicious criminal types

## 1 The Carbon-dioxide Crew

**Gang secret code** (as used by chemists): $CO_2$

**Description:** A carbon atom with two odious oxygen atom hangers-on.

**Criminal habits:** They're the Mr Bigs of the greenhouse-gas racket – they turn up like a bad penny whenever anything burns, rots or dies.

**Known haunts:** The gang has form. They get locked for years in trees and plants. Best place for them if you ask me! The cowardly crew also lies low in the sea.

**Known crimes:** When they escape from the sea or plants they make their way into the air and hang about for 100 years. They have been collared for causing over 25 per cent of global warming.

**Danger rating:** Poisonous to human beings – according to police boffins the gruesome gas can crowd out oxygen in the air so we suffocate. The public are urged to avoid this gang. (This is rather difficult as the public and every other animal breathes it out as a waste product of making energy.)

DON'T SAY WE DIDN'T WARM YOU!

## 2 The Methane Mob

**Gang secret code:** $CH_4$

**Description:** Evil-looking bunch of toughs aren't they? It's that carbon atom this time with a new crowd of cronies — four hydrogen atoms to be exact.

**Criminal habits:** They've been observed acting suspiciously around fossil-fuel mining, rice fields and rubbish dumps. They were creeping into the air — most likely up to no good.

**Known haunts:** Places where things are rotting — clearly they're a rotten crew. Known haunts also include animal and termite guts, where they're produced by microbes. My enquiries have revealed that cow belching and farting produces 200 litres of methane per day compared to 30 litres from sheep and 100 ml from humans — although some people produce more.

IT'S FART'OO SMELLY ROUND 'ERE!

Police intelligence reports vast numbers of gang members are lying low under the sea disguised as frozen deposits known as "methyl hydrates". More are said to have gone to ground — that's hiding under frozen ground in Arctic regions.

**Known crimes:** causing 9 per cent of global warming. Fortunately the Methane Mob are fewer than the Carbon-dioxide Crew and only hang about in the air for eight years.

**Danger rating:** Like the Carbon-dioxide Crew, these lethal louts have been known to elbow out the oxygen and prevent the rest of us from breathing — typical thuggish behaviour! The public are strongly advised not to sniff rotting rubbish. Since the gas is explosive, the public are also warned to extinguish all flames in the region of cows' posteriors.

### 3 Nitrous-oxide Duo

**Gang secret code:** NO
**Other alias:** Laughing Gas
**Description:** An oxygen atom teamed up with a nitrogen partner in crime. A highly dangerous combination if you ask me.

**Criminal habits:** Known to get together as a result of certain industries such as nylon making and farming with nitrogen fertilizers. Also made by lightning strikes.

**Known crimes:** Causes 300 times more global warming than carbon dioxide and also hangs about in the air looking for trouble for 100 years. Fortunately they're less common than carbon dioxide.

**Danger rating:** Well, there's a novelty – a villain with a social conscience! The NO gang turn up in hospitals doing "voluntary work" to dull pain. What's their game? That's what I'd like to know!

## 4 Lesser villains/small fry

Criminal elements such as the greenhouse-gas gangs attract hangers-on – and a thoroughly unpleasant bunch of misfits they are too...
They include:

### The Ozone Outfit

A tough trio of oxygen atoms – they're a renegade lot if you ask me. Up top in the atmosphere, they protect the law-abiding public from the Sun's harmful ultraviolet rays.

It's a pity they spoil all their good work by causing global warming closer to ground level. They appear when car exhausts react to sunlight, and they cause breathing problems for their innocent victims.

### Hydrofluorocarbons, perfluorocarbons and sulphur hexafluoride

Known to their criminal pals as the HFCs, the PFCs and the SFCs. These violently antisocial criminals hang out in the cooling mechanisms of fridges and the gas used in hairspray or flykiller aerosols. Personally I prefer cutting my hair short and swatting flies in the old-fashioned way.

Chief Inspector Gas-Bag was right to warn us about the perils of carbon dioxide. If the air was more than 10 per cent carbon dioxide, breathing would be deadly, (luckily there's less than 0.04 per cent at present). But the dangers of the gas were horribly proven in 1986. In that year thousands of people lived around Lake Nyos in Cameroon, Africa – all unaware that nature had turned the lake into a cruel killing machine…

Lake Nyos is an old volcano crater filled with water. But its dark, sinister depths are full of carbon dioxide from the volcano trapped under pressure like bubbles in your favourite fizzy drink. One night something – scientists aren't sure what – disturbed the lake. All at once, a giant gas bubble rose from the water and spread silently over the surrounding villages. That night 1,200 people were smothered in their sleep and their bodies were found covered in blisters caused by lack of oxygen damaging their blood vessels.

I'm going to say a lot more about carbon dioxide because this is the gas most experts like to gas about. It's so important that I'm going to call it "$CO_2$" from now on. Here's why it's so important. Leaving aside water vapour,

$CO_2$ is the gas that causes most global warming. What's more, it's the gas that we're doing most to pump into the air. The gas that we ought to control.

By the 2000s humans were puffing and burping more $CO_2$ into the air than ever. The grisly gas was increasing at the rate of 26 BILLION TONNES per year. That was four tonnes for every human on Earth.

That doesn't mean that each person actually puffed four tonnes of $CO_2$ into the air. Many people in poorer countries hardly produced any $CO_2$ and most of the gas was coming from people in richer nations doing the things that richer people like to do.

"So what might that be?" I hear you mumble. Well, let's go back to Choketown to meet the Guzzlers. They're doing more than their fair share for global warming, and here's how...

## MEET THE GUZZLERS

MR G    ENGLEBERT    EDWINA    MRS G

The Guzzlers produce greenhouse gas in the same ways as most families in richer countries – the only difference is that the Guzzlers produce MORE!

**1** Cars – the Guzzlers have NINE. That's one for Mr G, one for Mrs G and one spare for every day of the week. Each of their cars does about 1 km to a litre of petrol. The Guzzlers *always* travel by car – even if they just need to cross the road to post a letter.

**2** Home – their 42-room mansion is kept hot in the winter and if it gets too hot they open the windows. In the summer they have the air-conditioning on all the time and if gets too chilly they open the windows. All that energy uses loads of electricity and gas and releases lots of lovely $CO_2$. Meanwhile, Englebert and Edwina are trying to see who can leave the most lights and electrical devices switched on.

**3** Holidays – the Guzzlers love nothing better than jetting off to some beach on the other side of the world. Their plane trip will splurge 4 tonnes of greenhouse gas per person into the air. And the plane's vapour trail turns to clouds that trap even more heat.

**4** Work – Mr G is a supermarket boss. He's proud of the lights and air-conditioning and chiller cabinets and heating that go full blast even when the supermarket is closed. This uses masses of energy and blasts out $CO_2$. Mrs G works in the office and makes sure that all the office equipment is switched on even when it's not needed.

**5** Food – the Guzzlers love food – lots of it…
Fast food with lots of packaging. Packaging is great for global warming – it needs energy to make (releasing $CO_2$) and when it rots in a rubbish dump it releases more $CO_2$ and methane. Ready-made supermarket meals require lots of energy and packaging.

The family munches meat every day – just think of all the $CO_2$ and methane the animals make.

In the interests of healthy eating, Mrs G has persuaded the family to eat more fresh fruit and vegetables. The fruit and veg comes from Mr G's supermarket and naturally it's been flown thousands of kilometres. So there's a few more tonnes of greenhouse gas in that great big dustbin in the sky.

It's quite true that richer countries have the most well-travelled fruit and veg on the planet. Next time you visit a supermarket why not take a notebook and scribble down where the fruit and vegetables come from. I bet you'll find that much of it has had a long journey and dumped lots of $CO_2$ on the way. And even fruit and veg from your country has probably been driven hundreds of kilometres to be wrapped and packaged and sent out again to supermarkets.

**Bet you never knew!**
*In 2002 a British supermarket sold vegetables from Kenya, Africa, tied with a chive (a herb grown in Britain). Each chive had to be flown 13,600 km to Kenya to tie the veg and then flown back again. Isn't that nice? I bet all their herb friends were green with envy.*

No wonder we have a $CO_2$ problem!

Or do we?

In fact, a lot of $CO_2$ is produced naturally – for example, by microbes in the soil. The Earth deals with it because plants take in $CO_2$ and lock up the grisly gas for a while. What's more, a bit of global warming is *good* for us. Greenhouse gases keep our planet warm and without them your bedroom would be as cold as your freezer. But – and it's a MASSIVE BUT – the Earth can't handle the extra greenhouse gases from the Mighty Planet-Munching Machine…

So how do greenhouse gases warm our planet? Professor Large is trying to explain the science to Sam, but I think he's got more chance of melting the Antarctic with a box of extra-hot peppermints…

THE EARTH'S ATMOSPHERE IS 78 PER CENT NITROGEN AND 21 PER CENT OXYGEN. GASES THAT WARM THE PLANET ADD UP TO LESS THAN 1 PER CENT BUT THEY'RE HAVING BIG EFFECTS.

HERE'S THE GUIDE...

EH?

AND HERE'S THE IDIOT!

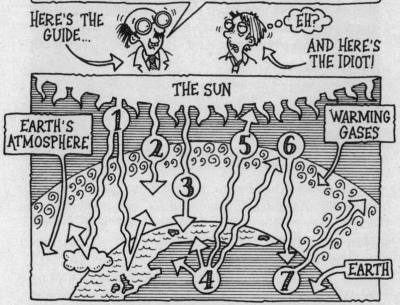

**1** 30 per cent sunlight reaching Earth reflects from clouds and dust and shiny seas and ice.

**2** 20 per cent soaked up by gases in atmosphere.

**3** 50 per cent soaked up by land and sea.

**4** Earth gives up the heat as infrared radiation. That's what you feel as heat.

**5** Some heat escapes into space.

**6** Some heat trapped in atmosphere by warming gases. This trapped heat warms up the planet.

**7** As the planet heats up, more greenhouse gas and water vapour is released to warm the planet even more.

The really horrible effects of global warming start to kick in when all this extra heat starts to waft around the planet. Let's step outside the Earth and go for a spacewalk...

See those arrows? They're the winds and ocean currents that help shape our climate. Unlike our weather they don't change much. Every year the winds and currents swirl about in much the same way – shifting heat and making sure that deserts stay dry and squishy areas get a good soaking. Trouble is, unlike your central heating the Weather Machine doesn't like people playing around with the thermostat. That's why nasty and unpredictable things start to happen when you turn up the heat.

What do I mean? Well, you get horrible heatwaves and dreadful droughts in some places and massive melting of ice and floods in others. Oh silly me, did I forget to mention the savage storms? It's going to take me the rest of this book to describe these dreadful details...

# HORRIBLE HEATWAVES

What's the hottest you've ever been? Well unless you've been stuck in an igloo at the North Pole, you've probably been hot enough to drip a few drops of sweat. And the chances are that you'll be losing quite a bit more squelchy stuff in the years to come. Want to know why?

Well, let's start with Professor Large's heroic attempt to explain heat to the human being who makes a potato look like mastermind…

### THE IDIOT'S GUIDE TO HEAT

WHAT IS HEAT — IS IT SOMETHING TO DO WITH EAT?

NO, SAM — IMAGINE A MOLECULE. NOW PLONK IT IN A FRYING PAN ON A COOKER. THE MOLECULE GETS HOT…

SO IT IS EAT! I BET YOU'RE COOKING IT WITH SOME TASTY SAUSAGES AND A FRIED EGG!

NO, NO, NO! THE MOLECULE WOBBLES FASTER AND FASTER AND PRODUCES INFRARED RADIATION. WELL, THAT'S HEAT — WOBBLING MOLECULES AND RADIATION.

THAT'S FASCINATING, PROFESSOR!

YES, BUT THERE'S NO NEED TO TRY THIS EXPERIMENT RIGHT NOW, SAM, GET OFF THE COOKER! I SAID… OH ALL RIGHT I'LL CALL THE FIRE BRIGADE.

I know very well that you're smarter than Sam – but how hot is your heat knowledge? Are you a sizzling scientist or just a little lukewarm?

## COULD YOU BE A SCIENTIST?

Eighteenth-century scientist Charles Blagdon (1748–1820) tested the effects of heat. He went into a room heated to 105°C – that's as hot as an oven – for 15 minutes. He took with him a dog, some eggs and a piece of raw steak. What happened next?

**a)** Not a lot. Baked Blagdon died and his eyeballs were cooked like hard-boiled eggs. You'll be delighted to learn that the dog survived and scoffed the steak.

**b)** Blagdon was fine but the dog was cooked. So the barmy boffin ate the dog.

**c)** Scientist and dog survived but the steak and eggs were cooked to perfection.

---

**Answer:**
**c)** The dog had to be put in a basket to stop its paws getting burnt. The scientist and the dog survived because their bodies had ways of keeping their temperature down.

---

I'm talking about what happens when you get too hot. Deep in your brain is a region called the hypothalamus. Amongst other jobs, your helpful hypothalamus monitors your blood temperature. If you're getting a bit roasted, it orders blood vessels in your skin to widen to lose heat. You also sweat, and as the lovely drippy sweat dries off your skin it takes heat with it.

Mind you, it's lucky that your body can cool itself. If it didn't you might start to suffer from headaches and confusion. People who get too hot actually stop sweating. Their skin turns pale and bluish and they may throw up or go blind. When their bodies get to 42°C brain damage can set in. At 45°C death is certain. And with that happy little thought let's check out why scientists are getting hot and bothered about the warming climate…

In 2007 scientists announced that eight of the ten hottest years ever recorded had happened in the past ten years. It's also known that average global temperatures had gone up 0.74°C in the past 100 years. It doesn't sound much, but dear old Planet Earth is a teeny bit sensitive to temperature changes. If you turn down the heating control by just 6°C you get this…

SNOWBALLS IN SPACE!!

That's right – another ice age. Turn up the heating by just 3°C and you could melt all the sea ice in the Arctic. Bye-bye polar bears.

IT'S A CHILLING PROSPECT!

Warmer temperatures don't guarantee heatwaves though. You need a really big city for that. Cities are hotter than the countryside because the roads and pavements and buildings suck up heat and let it out at night. This means that cities don't cool much in hot weather. Scientists call this "the heat island effect".

But not only are cities getting hotter – they're getting bigger too. In 1900 about 250 million or one quarter of all humans lived in cities. One hundred years later *half* the world's six billion people were city dwellers. What's more, the world's biggest cities are set to get even bigger. At this rate the heat islands will turn into heat continents.

Of course there have always been heatwaves. In the 1930s heatwaves in the USA did nasty things to the soil, but I'll tell you about that in the next chapter. Back in 1896 a New York heatwave killed 617 people and left the smelly streets full of dead horses. (They still used horses to get about in those days – today the streets would be full of dead cars.)

Today, with global warming looming larger and larger, it looks as if heatwaves are getting worse. Just look what happened to Europe in 2003. (You might like to pour yourself a long cold drink before reading this next bit.)

# THE DAILY W🌐RLD

July 2003

## IN TODAY'S ISSUE
- ☀ Sun – can we ever get enough?
- ☀ Sizzling fashion tips

## IT'S FUN IN THE SUN

Thanks to global warming Europeans have been enjoying their hottest summer ever.

Thousands are rushing to the Mediterranean beaches where the sea is as warm as a giant bath. Meanwhile ice cream and cold drink sales are soaring in the scorching sunshine.

We're getting reports of old folks dying in the heat. We at the *World* say keep an eye on Granny!

Old biddies don't sweat as much as us young 'uns so don't lock them in cars and give them a nice cup of tea to drink.

## OLDIES PEG OUT

# THE DAILY WORLD

August 2003

**HOT NEWS!**

## DEAD HEAT DISASTER!

We're cooked! Day after day the heatwave drags on and things are getting desperate! The editor's in his pants and string vest, our computers are melting and the office cat lives in the fridge! Can it get worse? Yes it can – the fridge has broken down!

People die in their sleep because they can't cool down. The elderly, kids and people in poor health are most at risk. In France 13,000 people have died and thousands more in Germany and the Netherlands. Many people are living in shopping malls – anywhere with air-conditioning. And now there's a new threat – pollution.

Car pollution is building up in the hot, still air and choking people. A leading scientist said, "The damage cough, cough, is being caused by ozone, wheeze, splutter, sulphur-based pollution sneeze and particles from car exhausts gasp help I need some oxygen!"

We don't know how much more of this we can take! We at the *World* say bring on the next ice age NOW!

**STOP PRESS!!!**
Paris morgues are packed with heatwave victims and now the bodies are stored in tents.

The scary thing is that thanks to global warming, some scientists reckon that this kind of killer weather will be hitting Europe *every other year.* Meanwhile the outlook for the USA and the rest of the world is just as baking. In 1995 one broiling week killed over 700 people in Chicago, USA.

Obviously, if you don't enjoy being slowly cooked in your own juices you might find this a depressing forecast. So what's to be done? Should we pay to send everyone to the seaside? Should we buy everyone air-conditioning? The trouble is, these ideas involve burning loads more energy and creating – you got it – more global warming. There has to be a better way … and it turns out that there is!

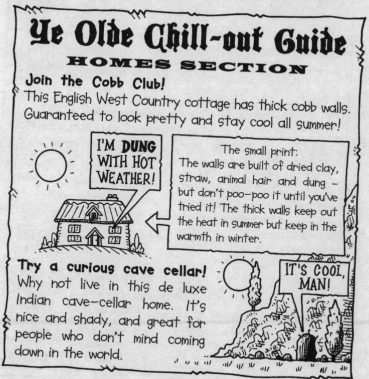

## Ye Olde Chill-out Guide
### HOMES SECTION

**Join the Cobb Club!**
This English West Country cottage has thick cobb walls. Guaranteed to look pretty and stay cool all summer!

I'M **DUNG** WITH HOT WEATHER!

The small print:
The walls are built of dried clay, straw, animal hair and dung – but don't poo-poo it until you've tried it! The thick walls keep out the heat in summer but keep in the warmth in winter.

**Try a curious cave cellar!**
Why not live in this de luxe Indian cave-cellar home. It's nice and shady, and great for people who don't mind coming down in the world.

IT'S COOL, MAN!

## Improve your home with traditional technology!

**NICE VIEW, TOO!**

This Japanese-style sliding wall will let a cool breeze waft through your home. (Just don't let anyone slide back the loo walls when you're inside!)

**WE'VE ALL GOT WIND!**

## Life's a breeze with a wind-catcher!

As used in Hyderabad, Pakistan, to scoop up a cooling draught...

## Change your routine!

Why suffer in the sun when you can snooze? Take a siesta in the roasty-toasty part of the day. The only problem is that you have to start work early and work later in the cooler part of the day.

**ZZZZ ZZZZ ZZZ!**

**NO SWEAT!** ## Dress to impress!

Don't peel off in the sun! You actually heat up quicker and you might peel some more – with sunburn! No, it's better to wear loose, light, Arab-style clothing to protect your skin whilst allowing cool air to circulate underneath.

*Bet you never knew!*
*Camels have their thickest hair on their backs for the same reason. The hair protects the camel from the sun and helps it to keep it cool. That's why if you give a camel a haircut it gets hotter and needs more water to drink.*

These traditional methods of staying cool really do work – and they're a lot better than a very silly British method tried in Africa and India in the 1900s…

# The Old Empire Magazine
## 1899

## STAY SAFE IN THE SUN

As everyone knows, invisible rays from the sun can penetrate your skull and spinal fluid and drive you mad. That's why you need the new improved COOL-BONCE sun-protection outfit – guaranteed to stop your brain from boiling…

METAL PLATE ON HAT TO BLOCK THE SUN'S RAYS

UMBRELLA FOR EXTRA PROTECTION

QUILTED MATERIAL ON SHIRT TO PROTECT SPINE

GOGGLES TO PROTECT EYES

HEESH, HEESH!

"My brain has never been so well-protected. I am sure the natives are jealous because they keep pointing at me and grinning."
*Colonel Bunbury-Bagshott, Africa*

Yes – you've guessed it. The invisible rays that drove people mad didn't exist. In fact you had to be mad to dress like that. Mind you, if heatwaves are driving you round the bend you'll be pleased to read that we're ending this chapter by a bright blue sea, white sands, swaying palm trees and all the coconuts you can eat. We're off to join Will D Beest and Mickey as they film their new TV series *Will's Wildlife*. Right now they're exploring a coral reef. Coral reefs are wonders of the world. They're built up from the skeletons of millions of small creatures called coral polyps. These beasties, live in a happy partnership with green microbes called algae. Now read on…

## WILL D BEEST IN … REEF GRIEF

So heatwaves are cooking coral reefs. In fact, the Mighty Planet-Munching Machine seems to have it in for coral reefs – they're being whacked by pollution, over-fishing and people selling tacky coral tourist souvenirs all at once. So the poor old polyps are in deep trouble. By 2008 over 16 per cent of the world's coral reefs had been destroyed.

Now, for the next chapter we're heading back to dry land. *Very* dry land…

# DREADFUL DROUGHTS

Have you ever heard people say "you can't have it both ways". What they mean is that you can't stay in bed half the day *and* go to the seaside, but global warming really does have two opposing effects. It makes the climate wetter *and* drier … at the same time! Not fair – is it?

### TEACHER'S TEA-BREAK TEASER

Summon up all your reserves of courage and beat out a cool rhythm on the staffroom door. When it swings open, confront your teacher with the following tricky question…

Most teachers haven't got a clue and with a bit of luck your teacher will start making gobbling noises and spill their mug of revolting school tea. In which case you can slip in the fatal follow-up question…

The correct reply is "yes" – and you'll probably see steam coming from your teacher's ears when you tell them the answer. Global warming makes the Earth hotter (but of course) and that means drought, as the hot air sucks water from plants and soil. But think of your teacher's tea. Heat turns the water into vapour – that's what you feel as moist air. There's plenty more water vapour in the air from the warming seas. As it rises, it cools and turns into clouds of water droplets just like the steam on your teacher's glasses. And guess what happens next? Rain – lots of it!

So that's why global warming can cause droughts *and* floods – it depends on where you live. But either way you can blame a naughty little boy… No, silly – I don't mean your little brother – I'm talking about something called an *El Niño* event. The name means "the little boy" in Spanish but it's really a glitch in the worldwide weather machine. Mind you, it's a good name – like a naughty boy, El Niño causes chaos, including droughts and floods.

**DEADLY DATA-BURST**
• Normally there's a large area of cool water off the coast of Peru, South America. Dry winds from this region keep the coast of South America dry.

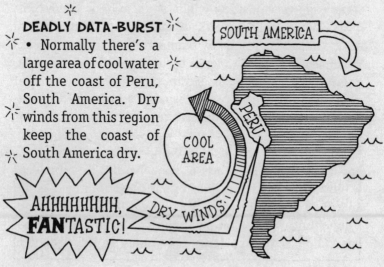

SOUTH AMERICA

PERU

COOL AREA

DRY WINDS

AHHHHHHHH, **FAN**TASTIC!

- During an El Niño event the winds change direction and warmer water replaces the cool area.
- The dry coast gets lots of rain (not to mention floods and mudslides) and knock-on effects with other weather systems cause widespread droughts...

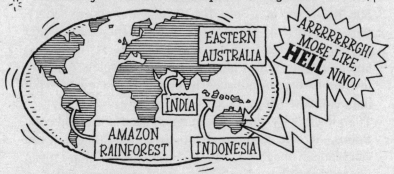

But the really bad news is that some scientists think that global warming is making El Niño events more powerful.

Drought spells misery for farmers. Not only do their crops wilt and wither, but the dry weather also makes some soils very dusty. A windy day can blow much of it away. Worse still, farmers in many parts of the world have damaged dry soils by planting crops such as wheat, which needs a lot of water or by letting cattle scoff all the grass. The result is a dust storm...

It's an ordinary day. As usual it's hot and dry, but what do you expect in a desert? You can't even remember the last time it rained. Maybe you've never seen a drop of rain in your whole life. Well, you won't today. A harsh hot, dry wind starts to spin the dust at your feet. It blows fine sand and grit in your face. Your eyes sting and dirt flicks your skin. Suddenly you don't feel safe – something bad is going to happen. You run but it's too late. There's a long, dark, dirty cloud in the distance.

It rolls and boils and tumbles towards you like a dreadful dry wave.

You cough and cover your mouth. Then it's all around you and you can't breathe. You're scared, you panic but you can't cry out. All you can see is dark and dirty yellow – then you can't see anything. All you can hear is the howling wind. And there's dirt in your eyes, nose and ears. Just in time you stumble into your house. There's dust in your house too.  You touch your face. Your skin feels sore and your eyes are gritty. Outside the yellow light is dim and scary. But you've been lucky – you've lived through a dust storm.

## DREADFUL DUSTY DETAILS

In the 1930s drought turned vast areas of the American Midwest into dusty disaster areas. Soil blew away and buried homes, and the dust caused deadly lung diseases. Helpless horses got buried alive. The dust covered the eastern USA and some even ended up on the president's desk.

In Australia in the 2000s drought linked to El Niño wiped out the wheat harvest and killed millions of unlucky sheep.

In Mongolia overgrazing by animals triggered huge dust storms that covered northern China in the 2000s.

Most tragically of all, Africa south and east of the Sahara has been hit time and time again by deadly droughts. Worsened by the effects of El Niño, overgrazing and war, the droughts have triggered famines that killed millions of people.

71

As usual, people are doing their best to tackle the trouble caused by drought – and, as usual, some of their efforts aren't exactly helpful. In a bid to stop soils drying out, farmers take water from rivers. But this drains the rivers and causes droughts in other areas. You need a really dry sense of humour to find this next bit funny...

## HORRIBLE HOLIDAYS PRESENT...
# Come to the Beautiful Aral Sea

We've got sun, sand and er, more sand...

☀ Enjoy the huge beaches of Asia's biggest lake – well, it was big once!

☀ Gasp at the sight of boats stranded many kilometres from water.

☀ Wonder where all the water went!

☀ Special prize for the first person to actually find the lake!

IT'S DESERTED, MUM!

GASP!

In the 1930s the rivers that fed the Aral Sea were diverted to irrigate cotton fields. Today the lake is only half its former size and the dried-up area is a salty wasteland. And that's not the only problem. When a river runs through more than one country, there can be heated rows when one nation tries to take more than its fair share of the runny stuff. Water load of fuss!

> **Bet you never knew!**
> In the 1930s Australian engineer Jack Bradfield had a brilliant brainwave. Why not flood the Lake Eyre region of Australia to make a lovely inland sea? The sea would moisten the air and make more rain. But experts decided that it wouldn't work and support for this drippy idea soon dried up.

A more sensible way to tackle water shortages is to do what people in dry countries have been doing for hundreds of years…

• Save water. Collect rainwater and use it to flush toilets or water plants. Reuse bath water in gardens too. Better still, use an earth loo, which turns poo and wee into non-smelly compost for the garden. And take showers – they use less water and energy.

ALL GROWN WITH OUR OWN POO AND WEE!

• Plant trees to protect the soil. In Niger, Africa, 200 million trees have been planted and they actually do keep the deserts at bay. And there's nothing new about this technique. In the 1900s the local Sultan of Zindar ordered that anyone who cut down certain trees would have their hands cut off. I guess it was a case of "hands off my trees!"

• Grow crops and raise animals that don't need much water. Plants that do well in dry conditions include millet, sorghum and chickpeas. Animals that don't get too thirsty include goats and certain breeds of sheep. Oh yes, and camels.

But even when humans try to fight droughts and deserts, global warming has another nasty surprise to spring on us – fire. When a forest or bushland is dry, even the tiniest spark sends them up in smoke. Forest fires aren't exactly new – trees such as the Australian bottlebrush and American lodgepole can't even grow from seeds until they've been burnt. But with El Niño on the rampage droughts are getting worse, and that means more fires than ever.

And more fires mean more burning, which means more $CO_2$ to cause more warming, which leads to more fires... What we need is a good downpour! Oh that's handy – it looks like there's one in the next chapter. And it's just sprung a leak...

# FATAL FLOODS AND SAVAGE STORMS

Every day, 300 billion tonnes of fresh water falls on the land. That's a lot – even if you drank like our thirsty camel friend it would take ten million years to drink it all. (Yes, scientists really have worked this out!)

As luck would have it, all this rain doesn't fall in one place – some areas get more of a soaking than others. I expect you think I'm talking about school sports days, outdoor entertainments and every place you've ever been on holiday. But I was actually thinking about places like these...

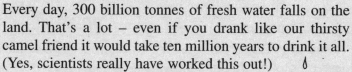

## HORRIBLE HOLIDAYS PRESENT...

### Get set for the wettest holiday ever!

Don't worry about rain on holiday – just enjoy it! We'll even give you a free umbrella and heavy-duty diving suit (you'll be needing them)!

**Make a splash!**
Come to romantic Cherrapunji, India. In just one year (1861–1862) this place enjoyed over 26 METRES of rain. Your holiday is sure to go swimmingly!

WE'LL BE BACK NEXT YEAR!

## That's shower power!

Lloro in Columbia has had over 13 metres of rain every year for the past 29 years. You won't feel a drip there – you'll feel lots of them!

EVERY CLOUD HAS A... **WET** LINING!

## Don't splash out on an expensive swimming pool!

Go to Reunion Island in the Indian Ocean. In 1952, 187 cm of rain fell in just two days. So if you want a swimming pool just open the door!

WELCOME!

## Don't be a fashion victim!

Why pay for expensive holiday clothes? Come and stay at Mount Waialeale in Hawaii. There's only five days in the year when it doesn't rain, so all you need are waterproofs and wellies!

OR PANTS!

What's that? You don't enjoy getting soaked to the skin and catching a cold? Oh dear – global warming is sure to bring loads more rain. This is partly due to our naughty little pal El Niño and partly, as I said earlier, because more heat means more water vapour. And that means more flooding. Scientists reckon that the number of days when there are more than 10 cm of rain or snow have increased by 10 to 15 per cent across most of the USA, Europe, Russia, South America and Australia (although Australia isn't that wet, as you know). In other words the climate is getting wetter and wet days are getting even wetter. It's a pity that the rain isn't splashing down on the drought-hit areas, but global warming isn't that thoughtful.

You get flooding where there's more water around than the land can soak up and the rivers can transport. As luck would have it, nature has a few nifty ways of stopping floods and here they are…

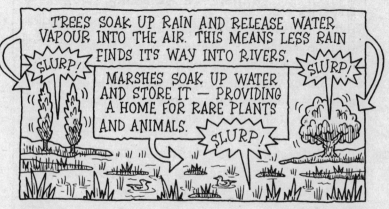

TREES SOAK UP RAIN AND RELEASE WATER VAPOUR INTO THE AIR. THIS MEANS LESS RAIN FINDS ITS WAY INTO RIVERS.

SLURP!

MARSHES SOAK UP WATER AND STORE IT — PROVIDING A HOME FOR RARE PLANTS AND ANIMALS.

SLURP!

SLURP!

## Dare you discover … how humans make flooding worse?

*You will need:*

Gloves

Measuring jug

Two old roasting dishes (Or you could use the same old dish and clean it out after each stage of the experiment.)

Some fertilizer or clean cat litter straight from the container

Some clean gravel straight from the bag

Two big books or phone directories

GRRR, WHERE'S IT GONE?

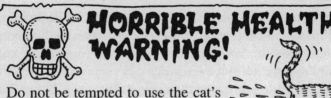
*What you do:*
**1** Check that any cuts on your hands are safely bandaged and put on your gloves.
**2** Fill one dish with fertilizer/cat litter. This is Dish A.
**3** Fill the other dish with gravel. This is Dish B.
**4** Prop each dish up on a book so it's on a slope.
**5** Fill the jug with 300 ml of water. Slowly pour the water on the top of Dish A and watch what happens.
**6** Then repeat step 5 for Dish B.

*You should find:*
A small pool may appear at the bottom of Dish A but it'll soon soak in. Dish B will flood more quickly.

*This is because:*
Soil will soak up rain – especially if there's not too much at a time. But Dish B is like human roads and houses that let rain run off fast, making floods more likely.

YOU HUMANS REALLY OUGHT TO PLANT MORE FORESTS AND PROTECT MARSHES.

WHAT A SENSIBLE POLAR BEAR!

Well, you might think so – but don't forget we're busy cutting down rainforests. And we're also draining marshes to build houses. You can guess the result. And floods kill people in quite a few interesting ways…

It's a sad fact that we humans die if we don't get enough water and we die if we're underwater too long. But the biggest danger in a flood isn't the water at all – it's cold. Just the shock of being chucked in cold water can disrupt the heartbeat and cause death. What's more, the shock can make the victim gasp even when they're underwater and that's no choke, er, joke.

Water cools a body 20 times faster than air and as they cool down the victim tends to gasp more. This reduces $CO_2$ levels in their blood, which makes it more alkaline. (Alkaline is the opposite of acid.) As a result their muscles can lock – which is a bad idea when they're supposed to be swimming. And even if they survive the cold the flood victim is still in danger. They could be dashed against rocks or other hard objects and end up in surprisingly small pieces.

There's worse in store when the waters drop. Water sneaks in where water isn't wanted – like electrical equipment or buildings that take months to dry out. And water has another horrible habit – it mixes with everything. This means the flood in your home isn't just water – it's a delightful brew of water, sewage, rotting rubbish, oil, mud and toxic waste. Nice.

Now I could tell you any number of terrible tales of foul and fearsome flooding, but here's just one. In 1966 nearly half a metre of rain fell in two days on Florence, Italy. Thanks to the felling of forests, the rain poured into the River Arno and swamped the city. Florence is one of the world's great treasure houses of art, but in 1966 it was a lake of sewage with priceless paintings floating about. The wild waters even trashed the tombs of famous Italians such as science superstar Galileo Galilei (1564–1642). And 159 people lost their lives.

## COULD YOU BE THE RAINING CHAMPION?

The power of rain has sparked many silly old stories but some might be true. Can you tell when these old folk are talking sense and when they're telling a shaggy dog tale…

a)

URGH!

I SAW A SHOWER OF BLOOD ONCE…

YOU MUST HAVE SEEN RED.

b)

EH?

I'VE SEEN A RAIN OF BONES AND SKULLS.

WAS IT DEAD FASCINATING?

c)

I WAS CAUGHT IN A RAIN OF FROGS LAST YEAR.

VERY FUNNY!

IT MUST HAVE BEEN FROGGY WEATHER.

**Answers:**
**a)** False – sorry to disappoint any vampires reading this book. Red rain is probably rain containing red dust and not blood!
**b)** True – this happened in New Orleans, USA, when a tornado trashed a cemetery.
**c)** True – there are lots of stories about rains of frogs or fish and they're probably caused by winds picking up water creatures and dumping them on land.

*Bet you never knew!*
*In 2002 panic reigned in Sangrampur, India. Buildings and people were splattered with sinister-looking green rain and many people thought they were the victims of killer chemicals. Then the state scientist tested the fearsome fluid and announced it was … bees' wee from a giant swarm.*

Mind you, if there's one thing worse than a giant swarm, it's a giant *storm*. And if there's one thing worse than a giant storm, it's a horribly HUGE storm known as a hurricane. And the YIKES WHERE'S MY PAIR OF WATERPROOF PANTS? news is that scientists believe that global warming makes hurricanes more powerful. Here's another deadly data-burst, and this one's a real blast…

## DEADLY DATA-BURST

• Giant storms go by different names in different oceans, but basically they're the same thing...

Hurricanes – in the Atlantic Ocean

Cyclones – in the Indian Ocean

Typhoons – in the Pacific Ocean

• Hurricanes develop at sea in areas north or south of the equator. The water has to be warmer than 27°C.

• With global warming the seas are getting hotter and so hurricanes are getting more powerful. This is because the more warm water there is, the more power the storm can pick up.

• The warm water results in moist air that causes thunderstorms. Next, the wind circles around an area known as "the eye". Can you spy the eye in this picture?

YOUR TURN, CAPTAIN...

SWIRL!

OK... I SPY WITH MY LITTLE EYE SOMETHING BEGINNING WITH... YARRRGH!

• Low air pressure in the eye causes the ocean to bulge under it. When the bulge reaches the shore it causes terrible flooding.

*Bet you never knew!*
*The custom of giving hurricanes names was started by our old pal Clement Wragge in the early twentieth century. It's said Clement named the killer storms after people he didn't like.*

**HURRICANE "NOISY NEIGHBOUR" HITS THE EAST COAST!**

*Today hurricanes get their names from an alphabetical list.*

Being stuck in a hurricane is about as scary as anything on Earth. In 1992 Hurricane Andrew hit Miami, Florida, and right in the middle were hurricane scientist Stan Goldenburg, his three sons and five relatives. Stan said, "We certainly wondered if we were going to live. We were in the most terrifying situation we could imagine."

The wind shrieked and the walls shook. All they could think of was the storm and their terror. With a rending roar the boards over their windows were ripped away and the glass shattered. Rain and wind blasted through the house. The terrified family tried to run to the car but there was no garage. As they huddled in the kitchen, the room filled with rain – there was no roof. Then a wall crashed down and nearly killed them.

Somehow they survived – but Hurricane Andrew killed 65 people and wrecked 25,000 homes.

## A BIT OF GOOD AND BAD NEWS

A bit of good news to do with tornadoes – I'm talking about the killer whirlwinds that caused that lovely shower of bones. Scientists say that global warming isn't triggering extra tornadoes.

And now some bad news to do with coasts. Remember how the hurricane made the sea bulge and flood the coast? It's called a storm surge. Savage storm surges have killed thousands of people. In 1900, for example, a hurricane storm surge smashed Galveston, Texas. The waves crashed over houses and killed 8,000 people. In 1970 a typhoon storm surge in Bangladesh killed up to half a million people.

Despite all this, for some reason everyone wants to live by the sea. In 1990 around a third of the world's people lived close to coasts but by 2002 this figure was 41 per cent and rising. Meanwhile, global warming was happily melting the world's ice and sea levels were creeping ever higher. So one thing is sure – there's worse flooding to come. The next chapter is certain to be cold … and wet.

# MASSIVE MELTDOWN

What's the most boring thing you have ever done?
• Counted the beans as you ate them cold from the tin?
• Spent the whole evening talking to a garden gnome?
• Sat through a science lesson without falling asleep?
Well, life doesn't come more tedious than watching ice melting, so it's no wonder most people aren't watching as the world's ice turns to water. But they should be – it's scary. We joined Will D Beest in the Arctic to check out the damage…

**WILL D BEEST IN … ARCTIC ADVENTURE**

85

Time for a few frozen facts…

### DEADLY DATA-BURST

• Most of the world's ice is found around the North and South Poles. In the north there's a frozen sea known as the Arctic Ocean and a frozen island – that's Greenland. To the south is the continent of Antarctica.

• Thanks to global warming, much of Antarctica is warming at the same rate as the rest of the Earth. At the edges of the super-chilled continent huge sheets of ice are breaking off into the sea.

• Meanwhile the Arctic permafrost – ground that stays frozen all year – is turning to goo. Houses and schools built on the permafrost are falling down. This means misery for homeowners and happiness for schoolchildren.

IT'S A BIT OF A **THAW** POINT!

SCHOOL

• Here's why scientists think the polar regions are warming faster than the rest of the planet. The troposphere is the lower layer of the atmosphere – it's where weather happens. Because the troposphere is thinner at the poles, the Sun can heat them up more quickly. What's more, ice reflects sunlight – remember that fact from page 55? And when ice melts, the darker ground underneath heats up quicker.

TROPOSPHERE – 8–10 KM THICK

TROPOSPHERE – 16–18 KM THICK

SWEAT! SWEAT! IT'S EVEN WORSE THAN WE **SPHERE**'D!

But it's not just the polar ice that's getting slushy. Many of the world's glaciers are melting too. Glaciers are awesome – they start off as snow falling on high ground and turn into awesome ice rivers. Glaciers tend to melt on lower ground, but as long as the snow keeps falling the glacier keeps moving. Some of them are thousands of years old. Once again global warming is doing the damage, by reducing snowfall and warming the grinding glaciers.

If you're not a glacier fan a few melting ice rivers won't put you in an icy sweat – but it should. Hundreds of millions of people throughout the world depend on glaciers for water supplies. And glaciers feed many of Asia's rivers, including the Ganges and the Yangtze. If the glaciers go the rivers will run dry in the summer and the crops that feed hundreds of millions of people will dry up too.

Not surprisingly, scientists are trying to save glaciers – but how? Well, you could do what one Swiss ski resort did with the Gurschen Glacier in 2005 and cover it with a giant insulating sheet to stop it melting. But this costs a lot of money. So why not make a new glacier? Here's a traditional method from Pakistan. The glacier provides villagers with water for their families and crops. Of course, it's just too bad if your school happens to be in the way...

# EVIL SCIENCE PROJECTS FOR BOYS AND GIRLS

## How to make your own glacier and crush your school under thousands of tonnes of ice!

Glaciers are pretty things, but an evil scientist like me is more interested in their raw destructive power. A glacier cave also makes a great hideout for an evil laboratory.

**Instructions:**

**1** You need an area under a semicircle of cliffs facing north-west and out of sunlight. The area should be covered in boulders about 25 cm across. (If there are no boulders you can order your army of slaves to drag them to the site.) Your chosen site should be above your school – you'll find out why in a moment.

**2** A bit of ice in the area would be a bonus – if not you might find buried ice. Order your slaves to cover the area of your glacier with 300 kg of snow ice. Any slaves who don't work hard enough should be turned into ice sculptures.

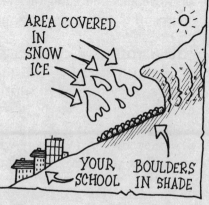

AREA COVERED IN SNOW ICE

YOUR SCHOOL

BOULDERS IN SHADE

**3** Now cover the snow with something to keep it cool – traditionally this might be charcoal, sawdust, nutshells or scraps of cloth. Or you might like to use school uniforms and shredded homework.

**4** Fill gourds of water and place them amongst the rocks and ice. As your glacier grows, the gourds will burst and freeze and make more ice. You may like to bury your enemies up to their necks in the frozen ground too.

**5** Every winter more snow falls on your glacier and it will get bigger. As it becomes heavier it will creep downhill and crush your school into matchsticks! That should put the cool back into school!

CRUNCH!

DOH! I'VE ONLY JUST BUILT THIS SCHOOL AFTER THE LAST ONE SANK INTO SOGGY PERMAFROST!

This method appears to work, although some spoilsport scientists reckon that the glaciers would just form anyway. Meanwhile, back at the coasts millions of tonnes of melting ice from glaciers and icy places such as Greenland are finding their way into the sea. Some ice breaks off to form giant icebergs…

## COULD YOU BE A COOL ICEBERG EXPERT?

In 1995 US scientists tried to capture a 30,000-tonne iceberg. They planned to smash the berg against a cliff to check out how strong it was. What do you think happened?

**a)** The iceberg drifted away with the unlucky scientists on it. They were never seen again.

**b)** The iceberg wouldn't shatter no matter how hard they tried.

**c)** The iceberg broke into bits before it could be tested.

**Answer:**
**1 c)** The first iceberg they tried broke up. A smaller berg shattered ... on the wrong cliff!

*Bet you never knew!*
*I know you won't believe this but in 2000 German scientists found a singing iceberg. It's true! The scientists discovered the talented iceberg in Antarctica. The delightful singing was caused by water rushing through the berg when it got stuck on the seabed. OK – the song was too low for human ears to detect, but when it was speeded up it sounded like a monster screeching in a horror movie.*

SCIENTIST LISTENING ON HIS 'ICE'POD

But hold on a minute, readers. I've just thought of something – what's our polar pal Clarence doing in Greenland? Well, I've got a sinking feeling and it's nothing to do with the permafrost. I reckon it's all to do with Professor Z's evil plot to rule the world...

## PROFESSOR Z'S EVIL PLOT TO RULE THE WORLD

The story so far... The sinister scientist and his equally evil assistant have collected a huge quantity of toxic waste and now they're in Greenland. We don't think they're here for the sunbathing...

But wait – is this possible? Could Greenland really melt and cause massive flooding? Yes it could, and here's an experiment to show how Greenland's melting could put the rest of us in hot water (well, fairly cool water, actually)…

## Dare you discover ... how melting Greenland could raise sea levels?

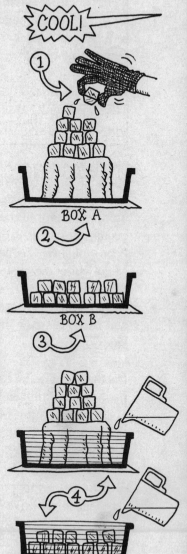

*You will need:*
Two small plastic boxes –
try using the kind of boxes
that takeaway foods come in
Jug of water
2 paper towels
Gloves
Ruler
Plasticine or modelling clay
24 ice cubes
Measuring jug

*What you do:*
**1** Pull on your gloves before handling ice or it could burn your hands.
**2** Make the modelling clay into an island and put it in one of your boxes – the island has to be higher than the sides of the box. Then pile 12 ice cubes on top of it. You can call your island "Greenland" if you like but I'll call it Box A. You could call the other box "Arctic Ocean" but I'll call it Box B. Place each box on a paper towel.
**3** Scatter 12 ice cubes in Box B.
**4** V-e-r-y slowly pour water into each box until it's bulging at the brim. Easy does it now – you don't want to spill any water on the paper towels!

93

**5** Wait for the ice to melt – this might take a night. Oh well, cheer up, scientists think it might take 300 years for all the ice in Greenland to turn slushy.

**6** When the ice has completely melted compare how damp the paper towels are.

*You should find:*
The towel under Box B is dry and the towel under Box A should be soggy. When the ice in Box B floated, it shoved aside its own volume of water. That's what happens when anything floats – an ice cube, an ocean liner or your auntie Flo in a swimming pool. When the ice melted in box B the water didn't rise any higher because it had already been pushed aside. Meanwhile the water from the ice in Box A ran into the water and dribbled over the sides of the box.

It's the same in the real world. As global warming gathers pace, the Arctic sea ice is melting – but because the ice is already floating the sea level doesn't alter*. But if all the ice in Greenland melts, it would raise the sea level by 7 metres – that's enough to cause massive flooding and grief to millions of people.

*Important science note
Even without melting ice, sea levels would still rise a bit. That's because as seas warm up the molecules move apart more.

So who might be hit hardest? Well, any low-lying area close to the sea could be in line for a soaking. Take Florida, for example. Rising sea levels could swamp the swamps and cover coastal cities. That means no more holidays and the alligators will have to find somewhere else to live. Meanwhile in Bangladesh 30 million people live on land that could be underwater if there's even a 1-metre rise in sea level. They're already in danger from typhoons – rising sea levels will make things worse. But if that sounds bad, just wait until you visit these places...

## HORRIBLE HOLIDAYS PRESENT...

If you like seaside holidays you'll lurve to get really close to the waves. That's really, really close to the waves. Well, in them, probably...

### You won't shiver at Shishmaref!

Shishmaref, Alaska, used to be ringed by boring ice. But thanks to global warming the ice is melting. Now the waves smash the shore and wash away at the low-lying village. This makes every storm an adventure!

WAVE!

**Stop Press** – We've just heard that the village was abandoned in 2004. Oh well, never mind there's always...

# ~ Toodle-oo Tuvalu! ~

Come to the Pacific paradise of Tuvalu before it's too late! The diving is great, and because it's just above the waves you'll be doing rather a lot of diving. And if the tide gets too high you can "wave" goodbye to Tuvalu!

WATCH YOUR KIDS SWIM FROM THE COMFORT OF YOUR LIVING ROOM

In fact thousands of low-lying islands are facing a watery fate. Many are protected by coral reefs. Well, they were protected by coral reefs until the Mighty Planet-Munching Machine started wiping them out.

As it is, the future for these island people and all those millions who live close to coasts is grimmer than an ice sculpture in a heatwave. But will the future really be that bad? Well, no – actually it could be a lot worse. See ya in the next chapter!

READ ON IF YOU DARE...

# FATEFUL FORECASTS

Everyone watches the weather forecast – but just imagine that one day it forecasted the end of the world?

But is the future really that grim or am I just trying to make your hair stand on end? Well, forecasts change and scientists disagree about the details, but the big picture is clear. And right now it's being discussed at a conference of top scientists and world leaders. Will D Beest is about to make a speech…

I'M WILL D BEEST THE TV NATURALIST (NO AUTOGRAPHS PLEASE) AND THIS IS MY PET, MICKEY...

PET? I LIKE TO SEE MYSELF AS AN EQUAL PARTNER, ACTUALLY.

AS A FAMOUS TV PRESENTER I GET TO FLY ALL OVER THE WORLD...

YAWN!

I BET THAT DOES WONDERS FOR GLOBAL WARMING

WHILST FILMING MY LATEST SERIES, "WILL'S WILDLIFE", TO BE SHOWN ON CHANNEL 1 AT 8 PM, I SAW THE DEVASTATION CAUSED BY GLOBAL WARMING AND HAD TO FIGHT OFF A WILD POLAR BEAR WHO WAS STARVING BECAUSE THE ICE WAS MELTING...

WILD? WELL YES, I WAS RATHER PUT OUT...

YEAH!

Oh dear, I don't think Will is going to finish his speech. But he was going to say that global warming is wrecking habitats – these are the places that plants and animals live. Scientists forecast that by 2050 we'll have wiped out a quarter of all plants and animals. Sounds bad? Well, that assumes we go easy on the $CO_2$. If we burp $CO_2$ faster we could destroy 70 per cent of all the life on the planet…

But why?

Well, the big problem is that Earth is warming too fast for nature to keep up. Plants and trees can't get up and walk to cooler regions and when they die the animals that depend on them lose food and shelter. Meanwhile, as global warming heats up, there's worse news in the pipeline for our coral polyp pals. As if pollution, overfishing and overheating aren't enough to spoil a polyp's day, scientists reckon that by 2100 the seas will be more acid than they have been for 100,000 years. This is worrying for the coral creatures and any other sea animal with a shell. They need a substance called carbonate to make their shells and this is harder to do in more acid water.

If I was an animal I'd be growling about this, so it's not surprising that Nature-Net (the Internet for wildlife) has been getting some angry emails from brainy beasts…

**Hi All**
I'm not warming to these hot nights we're getting. They spread a fungus that's bumping off my babies.
Yours A. Golden-Toad
(South America)

**Hi Everyone**
I'm shattered! Humans have ripped out the hedges where I used to sleep. And thanks to global warming I've got heat stress in the summer and it's too warm to sleep in the winter. Anyone got any sleeping pills?
Yours A. Dormouse
(Britain)

**Hi-ya**
I love the cool high life – that's why I live in mountains under snow. Er, so where's the snow and why are my mountains so hot?
Yours A. Pika
(USA)

Hiya Gang!
Give humans a break! We lurve those juicy scraps of festering fly-blown food they leave out for us. And we want to say THANKS for milder winters that help more of our babies survive! Keep up the good work you lovely two-leggers!
Love the Rat Family
PS Anyone know a nice toilet we can move into?

Hi Fellow-Munchers!
Thanks to good old global warming we're moving into cooler areas to gobble up all those unsightly potato fields! And what's more, the humans won't have to eat all those nasty unhealthy crisps! It's just our way of showing love.
Love the Colorado Beetles

In fact there's a horrible horde of bloodthirsty bugs ready to rampage into cooler climates and chew up our crops and share their deadly diseases with us. Back at the conference the next speaker is describing scary scenarios. But then he's always happiest when he's being depressing. Meet Dr H Grimgrave, the world's most dismal doctor…

And finally, of course, we come to global warming itself. How is the planet-wide warming and wild weather going to develop? Can it really get warmer and wilder? Should we stay in bed tomorrow morning?

## FATAL FORECASTS - THE REALLY SCARY BITS

Before I tell you what the scientists are saying I wanted to explain how the boffins can tell what the climate will be like in 20 years time when the weather forecast didn't get it right this morning. It's all to do with data…

### DEADLY DATA-BURST

• Scientists measure changes in greenhouse gases over thousands of years by drilling deep cores of the ice in Greenland and Antarctica. They've dug out ancient ice over 650,000 years old (almost as old as the fossilized frost at the back of your teacher's fridge). The ice contains trapped ancient air, including greenhouses gases.

• Satellites exactly measure the changing temperature of the sea and land, and map rising sea levels and melting ice.

• Supercomputers can predict how changes in greenhouse gases and temperature will affect the climate in the future.

• All the data tells the same story. The increase in greenhouse gases matches the rise in temperature.

*Bet you never knew!*
*Scientists have known that $CO_2$ was linked to global warming since Victorian times. In fact Swedish scientist Svante Arrhenius (1859–1927) figured that doubling $CO_2$ would cause a 5–6°C jump in temperature. (Modern experts think it's a bit less.) But he didn't take it too seriously – he reckoned the big warm-up would take 3,000 years and a warmer world would be quite nice.*

At the conference, Professor N Large is explaining how scientists think the climate will change…

GREENHOUSE GASES ARE AT THEIR HIGHEST LEVELS FOR 650,000 YEARS. BY 2100 WE EXPECT A 1.1° – 6.4°C RISE IN TEMPERATURE DEPENDING ON HOW MUCH EXTRA GREENHOUSE GASES WE PRODUCE. THE WORLD'S ICE WILL CONTINUE TO MELT AND THE SEA LEVEL COULD RISE BY AT LEAST 59 CM…

**A note for anyone who likes their science really complicated**

Just to confuse you – many scientists think that melting Greenland ice could weaken the Gulf Stream. This is a current in the North Atlantic that supplies north-eastern USA and Europe with warm water and takes cold water towards the equator. If the Gulf Stream stutters, Europe and the USA will get a bad case of the chillies. So global warming could result in freezing winters! It's always nice to have something to look forward to…

But just when you think things could be worse – they get worse. It turns out that the climate of our small blue planet is like a house of cards… It may look stable but there are a whole lot of vicious circles ready to wreck it. A vicious circle is nothing to do with a nasty maths problem. It's when something bad happens and triggers something else that makes the first bad thing worse. Remember how warming releases water vapour and $CO_2$ that triggers more warming? Well, that's just the start. Imagine you're a mad scientist like Professor Z, dedicated to destroying civilization…

## How to destroy civilization in 8½ easy stages

**1** Clear the kitchen table and put the cat out.

**2** Make sure you have everything you need. You'll need one small blue planet known as Earth and about six billion silly people to help you.

**3** Burn as much fuel as you can to release $CO_2$. Your planet will warm up and you'll see lots of water vapour rising up to make things hotter.

> PUT MORE COAL ON THE FIRE

> PASS ME THE MATCHES…
> …AND MY AXE!

**4** A drought will kill off the rainforests. Make sure they burn and release loads more $CO_2$ into the air. Feel free to cut down the rainforests too – they only spoil the view.

**5** As the soil of your planet warms up, microbes will work harder to rot plants and let more $CO_2$ into the air. Your planet is sure to warm up even more.

ROT! DECAY!

**6** This will melt all that nasty ice and raise sea levels. The permafrost contains huge amounts of methane – 70 billion tonnes in Siberia alone. As the ice melts the methane escapes to warm your planet even more.

**7** Greenland melts and the western part of Antarctica collapses into the sea. Vast floods destroy many of Earth's coastal cities. Drought, famine, floods and disease spread over the globe.

**8** Congratulations! You've won – it's the end of civilization as we know it!

**8.5** Watch it all on the TV news.

OOPS – TV SETS DON'T SEEM TO BE WORKING ANY MORE!

Actually, it's a bit more complex than that. Steps 2 to 6 happen at the same time, and just to keep you awake at night, the methane is escaping from melting permafrost right now. Scientists call these vicious circles "positive feedback" – but they don't sound very positive to me.

The truly terrifying thing about global warming is that even if we stop burping out $CO_2$ tomorrow these fearsome feedbacks will go on warming the planet. What's more, if we warm the planet by more than 2°C the climate is going to behave like a car going over a cliff. You jam on the brakes but nothing happens. By then global warming will be unstoppable.

If this happens it's hard to imagine anyone living happily ever after. But will it? Will we end up living in caves and munching mouldy potatoes that the beetles didn't want?

You're about to find out!

## HOW TO SAVE THE WORLD AND MAKE POTS OF MONEY

Back at the conference, the scientists are getting excited – everyone wants to save the world and everyone has a plan to do it…

We've taken all the ideas that people have suggested and placed them in three piles.

Of course you might not agree with which idea goes where, and some of the silly ideas might prove to be sensible – we'll just have to see!

We'll start off with an extremely silly idea from a Very Important Politician…

WHY DON'T WE DO NOTHING AND WAIT FOR THE OIL TO RUN OUT?

This idea is extremely silly for two reasons. First, there's enough coal, gas and oil knocking around to wreck the planet and second, even when the fossil fuels run out some scientists are working flat out to find new fuels to burn and release more $CO_2$. Some of them are thinking about using all that methane from the Arctic or under the sea.

*Bet you never knew!*
*In recent years scientists have experimented with some interesting new fuels.*

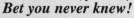

THANKS, FELLA!

*1 In 2006 a San Francisco company planned to collect doggie poo and feed it to microbes to make methane fuel. They could even do this with human poo – it sounds a rotten idea.*

*2 Another company planned to make oil from a mix of water, minerals, nitrogen fertilizer ... and turkey guts.*

YIKES! IT SOUNDS WORSE THAN CHRISTMAS!

HOW **UDDER**LY RIDICULOUS!!

*3 In 2005 Swedish scientists developed a train powered by methane. The gas came from rotting cow guts. Would you have the guts to work on this project?*

## STRANGE PLANET-SAVING IDEAS QUIZ

Which of these is genuine?

**1** Scatter loads of iron filings on the ocean. They'll boost the number of microscopic creatures called plankton that take in $CO_2$.

**2** Spray loads of seawater into the air to reflect sunlight and cool the Earth.

**3** Fill the upper atmosphere with tiny bits of metal to reflect sunlight.

**4** Plonk a giant lens the size of Western Europe in space to block sunlight.

**5** Scatter moondust in space to block sunlight.

**6** Cover Earth's major cities with special glass domes that reflect heat.

I'LL TRY THEM ALL – JUST HURRY UP AND DO SOMETHING!

**Answers:**

**1** TRUE – but in a 2009 test the extra plankton were scoffed by selfish shrimp.

**2** TRUE – but the salts from the water might stop rain forming and cause droughts.

**3** TRUE – it was suggested by scientist Edward Teller (1908–2003). I bet he took a shine to the idea, but it could damage the ozone layer.

**4** TRUE – it sounds fine, but it might be bad news for plants.

**5** TRUE – but moondust is quite shiny so when it's not blocking light it might be reflecting more sunlight to Earth.

**6** FALSE – as far as I know!

All these ideas share the same basic flaw – even if they worked they would need huge amounts of energy to turn them into reality and that means … more global warming! And talking about problems, look who's gatecrashed the conference!

## PROFESSOR Z'S EVIL PLOT THE RULE THE WORLD

TO BE CONTINUED...

## FAIRLY SENSIBLE IDEAS

Alongside the bad ideas and the out-and-out impractical ideas, scientists and world leaders are looking at some fairly sensible ideas.

Here's the most obvious – why don't countries put limits on the $CO_2$ going up in smoke? Well, they're trying. Trouble is, the same countries want to make money from the Mighty Planet-Munching Machine and they're not keen to cut their $CO_2$ more than another country. It's a bit like calling a meeting and asking people to limit their breathing.

Never mind, in 1997, world leaders agreed at Kyoto, Japan, to cut the amount of $CO_2$ from the air by 5.2 per cent of 1990 levels. Good news? *Hmmm.*

It took until 2006 for enough countries to agree to the Treaty so it could come into force. And even then the USA – the biggest $CO_2$ polluter – didn't want to sign up. Meanwhile the Earth got warmer, sea levels got higher and polar bears got sweaty. Then scientists realized that a 5.2 per cent cut was pathetically puny given the scale of the problem…

Still, the deal was better than nothing and there have been results. Companies and countries are trading carbon credits – these are the rights to put $CO_2$ in the air. The idea is you cut the $CO_2$ you pump and sell your rights to naughty people who still want to burp the grisly gas into the atmosphere. So in theory, saving $CO_2$ can make you rich.

What's more, by 2008 teams of scientists were working together to share data on global warming in organizations such as the IPCC (International Panel on Climate Change). So now we can discover how bad things are getting.

## TIME FOR ANOTHER QUITE SENSIBLE IDEA

Remember how oil and gas were disappearing down the global plughole? Well, scientists are looking for new kinds of fuel that won't boost global warming – and I'm not talking about doggie poo... I mean power sources that *don't* involve burning and so don't burp $CO_2$ into the air...

The more sensible forms of power include renewables. That means using energy from winds, waves, sun and falling water to produce electricity. The great thing about them is that you don't need to dig up the energy – it comes free with the weather. In fact renewables are perfect apart from the embarrassing fact that the sun doesn't usually shine 24 hours a day and the wind doesn't blow non-stop but we need electricity on demand. Big hydroelectric power stations do produce power all the time using the energy from waterfalls, but there's a problem. The waterfalls often need huge dams that can harm the environment. Still, by storing the electricity – perhaps in new forms of battery – renewable energy could be a great help.

*Bet you never knew!*
*Another approach is to build coal power stations that remove $CO_2$ and bury the unwanted stuff in old oil wells or salt mines. Hmm – could this be another use for a useless old school?*

SHUT THE WINDOW, JENKINS!

Also in the new-power A-list are hydrogen power and nuclear power. Hydrogen power is OK, but to use this light, easy-burning gas as fuel you have to make it and move it, and this needs lots of energy and new pipes and a lot of other big, expensive $CO_2$-boosting changes.

As for nuclear power, it's not every scientist's cup of tea. Come to think of it, if you had a cup of nuclear tea you might need a new set of insides. The basic idea of nuclear power is great. Radioactive uranium atoms break down and give out heat. So you use the heat to make lots of $CO_2$-free electricity. What's wrong with that?

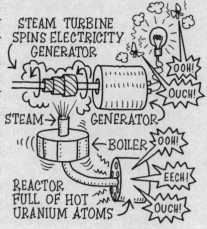

Well, people do tend to worry about nasty accidents such as the one that happened at Chernobyl, Ukraine, in 1986. A blast at this nuclear power station killed 56 people, caused thousands of cases of cancer and created a vast no-go area. What's more, no one knows how to store the radioactive nuclear waste safely for thousands of years or how to clear up the area when a power station closes down.

Oh well, if you can't make more power you can make sure the power you have goes further. That's why car and plane makers are busy designing new cars and planes that need a bit less fuel and cause a bit less global warming.

The new cars are also set to run on new fuels. In 2008 governments were very keen to see the new cars powered by biofuels. The idea is that you grow plants such as sugarcane, maize, palm-oil trees, even some types of grass, and use microbes to ferment them into ethanol – the posh scientific name for alcohol. In other words, you can run the family run-about on the boozy by-product. What's more the carbon in the biofuel came from $CO_2$ already in the air, so growing biofuel helps to fight global warming.

Nice idea – and by 2008 sugarcane biofuel powered 30 per cent of cars in Brazil. But biofuels come with a pocketful of prickly problems…

Hungry poor people aren't exactly over the moon when the cost of maize goes up because the sweetcorn they were hoping to eat for supper has been turned into fuel for gas-guzzling motors.

And rainforests aren't improved by being flattened for palm-oil plantations.

Biofuels could mean more roads and more cars and that means more work for the Mighty Planet-Munching Machine, and more global warming.

Maybe it would be more sensible to power down the machine that's causing global warming?

## SOME SERIOUSLY SENSIBLE IDEAS TO SAVE THE WORLD

Many scientists and non-scientists think the answer could be a low-energy lifestyle. Now I bet you think that means staying in bed half the day and being too lazy to do your homework…

Sorry. Low energy means using as little power as possible and saving as much energy as possible in order to limit the amount of $CO_2$ getting into the air. This may sound grim, but it doesn't mean living in a wigwam, taking cold baths and munching lentils for breakfast. And you won't have to wear an embarrassing itchy jumper, recycled underpants or hug a tree either.

What it does involve is a new lifestyle. It means not wasting energy, trying to travel as little as possible, and taking a new approach to food. This might sound ambitious but millions of people are doing low-energy things already – and that might include your family. And most people in poorer countries have never lived any other way.

I bet you think you can't live a low-energy lifestyle and be still be well-off. Well, we've recruited four volunteers to show you the low-energy lifestyle in action. Let's meet the Guzzler family!

Pause for gasps of shock from readers. Yes, readers – as a result of reading this book the Guzzlers have become born-again energy-savers! And there have been big changes at the Guzzler mansion…

MEET OUR NEW TENANT!

1 The house now has top-of-the-range-insulation and triple-glazed windows to keep the cold out and save energy.
2 The house has low-energy light bulbs and all the gadgets are ultra-low energy.
3 The Guzzlers have a new type of fuel-cell boiler

*Scientists and architects are experimenting with new house designs that don't use any energy at all. Take the German "passive house" for example...*

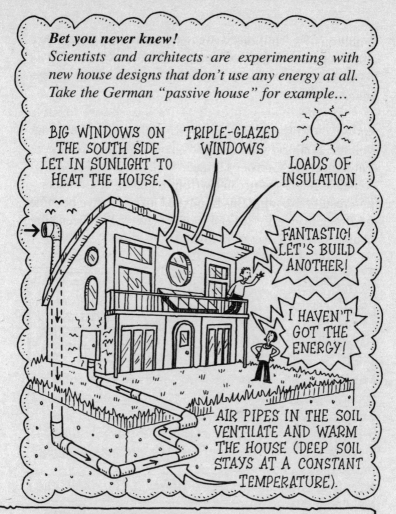

BIG WINDOWS ON THE SOUTH SIDE LET IN SUNLIGHT TO HEAT THE HOUSE.

TRIPLE-GLAZED WINDOWS

LOADS OF INSULATION.

FANTASTIC! LET'S BUILD ANOTHER!

I HAVEN'T GOT THE ENERGY!

AIR PIPES IN THE SOIL VENTILATE AND WARM THE HOUSE (DEEP SOIL STAYS AT A CONSTANT TEMPERATURE).

invented in the 1990s. It uses the heat it makes to produce electricity.

**4** They've also got $CO_2$-free solar panels to make more electricity from sunshine and a wind-turbine.

**5** The rooms the family don't use have been let to tenants – bringing in a tidy income and cutting fuel bills.

A house that heats itself for free – how good is that? Hopefully one day every house will be like this – and every school and factory too. Meanwhile, back at the Guzzlers' mansion…

**1** The Guzzlers have sold their nine cars (for recycling) and are getting along very nicely thank you with just one… It's an electric car that uses a battery recharged by the Guzzlers' garden wind-turbine and solar panels.
**2** The car produces no pollution and no $CO_2$, and because it gets its power from the sun and wind it doesn't cause global warming. It's not as fast as the Guzzlers' old cars but it's fine for what they want.

Mind you, old habits die hard, and Mr G is thinking about getting a new car. He can't wait for solar-powered cars to come on to the market.
**3** These days the Guzzlers travel as little as possible. Mr Guzzler uses new video-conferencing Internet technology to take part in business meetings from home and the family do most of their shopping on the Internet. That way they can save time, money and energy because everything is delivered.

**4** What's more, the family are about to save even more money. They love seaside holidays, but this time they're going somewhere closer to home. And they're going by coach to save fuel.

**5** It's often said that you are what you eat – but it's also true that you are what you throw away. So if you discard a lot of rubbish… As part of their low-energy lifestyle, the Guzzlers are chucking less and recycling more. They have separate bins for paper, plastic, metal and glass, and they dump their vegetable peelings in a compost bin. When they buy things for the house they often visit local second-hand shops to pick up classic antiques – although some of the things they come back with might make you cringe.

**6** Guzzler's Supermarket has also had a makeover. Well, for one thing, it's not a supermarket anymore. It's a warehouse for fresh local foods – selling over the Internet. People phone or email their orders and Mr G's fleet of electric vans delivers. And because he doesn't need to spend a fortune on heating and lighting and cooling, Mr Guzzler's bills have crashed through the floor, which means he can sell cheaper foods than the supermarkets and pay farmers a fair price – and still make pots of money.

**7** The new, environmentally friendly Mr G is keen to help organic farming. That's a way of farming that doesn't use any energy-intensive, $CO_2$-burping, wildlife-zapping pesticides. Instead it uses traditional farming methods to help wild animals and keep unwanted bugs and weeds at bay. In fact, the family tries to eat organic food as often as they can – but not too much meat. After all, animals bred for meat use more energy than plants (not to mention the effects of their musical methane-burping backsides).

YEAH! EAT MORE VEGETABLES – THEY'RE GOOD FOR YOU... **AND US!**

**8** As a result of their healthy diet and walking more, the little Guzzlers are fitter and have more energy. And the family will enjoy better health for the rest of their lives.

FULL OF FATNESS    FULL OF FITNESS

*Bet you never knew!*

*Scientists have worked out which funerals use less $CO_2$. Big steel-lined tombs are the worst. All that steel uses lots of energy – each year in the USA building de luxe graves produces the same amount of greenhouse gas as 200,000 cars. Cremation (burning the body) isn't much better – just think of all that fuel. No, according to scientists it's more planet-friendly to push up the daisies in a cardboard coffin in a wood. That way the body's $CO_2$ can end up in a tree.*

Well, hopefully getting buried in a low-energy funeral isn't top of your wish-list right now, but I guess making money could be. Did you notice how much lovely loot the Guzzlers were saving? Wouldn't you just love to grab your share? Low-energy can mean high-income so pin back your eyeballs – here's how to do it…

### Dare you discover … how to save energy and make money?

*You will need:*
An electricity or gas bill
A gullible parent
An innocent smile
A calculator

*What you do:*
**1** Wait until your gullible parent opens their bill. Soon afterwards you'll hear strange grinding sounds (that's their teeth gnashing together). If the bill is especially big they may turn pale and make a pitiful bleating sound. Choose your moment carefully and make them an offer they can't refuse…

122

Point out that this arrangement will cost them nothing since they will be saving the money, and it will actually leave them better off. And if that doesn't convince them, look rather sad and say:

What's that? You've sealed the deal? Great!

**2** Go around the house and switch off all equipment on standby. This includes TVs, computers, CD players, playstations and washing machines. (Don't turn off fridges or freezers or you might get a frosty reaction from your parents.) Good news – you've just sliced seven per cent off your fuel bill – that's 3.5 per cent for you and you haven't even started!

**3** Turn down the thermostat by 1°C to cut up to 10 per cent off the bill. And turning the thermostat down by 12°C when you are going away will save even more. Next, turn down the water temperature on the boiler to no more than 50°C. (You'll need adult help for this – blowing up the boiler won't do much for your money-making schemes.

OOPS, SORRY DAD... BUT HEY, NOW WE CAN REPLACE IT WITH A SUPER-EFFICIENT BOILER!

**4** The average house has 23 lightbulbs. Insist that your parent replaces the lot with low-energy bulbs. Point out that energy-saving bulbs are an investment that will save your parent money.

**5** Write down a new set of house rules:

## New House Rules

**1** No lights or electrical equipment to be left on in empty rooms.

**2** Baths are banned. Smelly parents and brother/sisters are allowed to take showers instead.

OR, YOU CAN JUST STAY DIRTY!

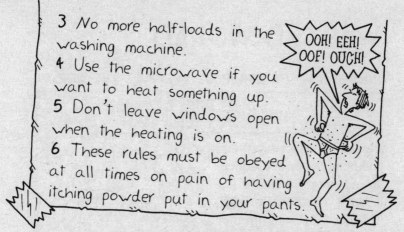

3 No more half-loads in the washing machine.
4 Use the microwave if you want to heat something up.
5 Don't leave windows open when the heating is on.
6 These rules must be obeyed at all times on pain of having itching powder put in your pants.

OOH! EEH! OOF! OUCH!

You may need to patrol the house to put out lights and switch off TVs that no one is watching but it'll be worth it. The fuel bills will be cut and there'll be an avalanche of cash rolling your way. Saving the planet AND making money – now that can't be bad! And what's more it's the first step to a low-energy lifestyle!

But will it be enough?

Humans created the Mighty Planet-Munching Machine – but can we control it? Or is it too late? And oh dear, I've just remembered something – Professor Z said he was going to flood the world with toxic waste in ten minutes and that was nine and a half minutes ago!

Are we about to get wasted?

YOU BETTER BELIEVE IT!

# WASTED WORLD

## PROFESSOR Z'S EVIL PLOT THE RULE THE WORLD

Typical mad scientist! Just because we won't let him rule the world he gets into a strop and blasts off in his private space rocket. Oh well, time to sum up this book.

Let's go back in time. It's 251 million years ago and everything is quiet. The seas are ruled by giant fish and the land is ruled by chunky reptiles. There are no dinosaurs yet and no humans. Then one day the earth opens up in Siberia and vast volcanoes spew out awesome amounts of $CO_2$. The grisly greenhouse gas heats the Earth and the temperature soars 6°C – far hotter than it is now. The heating kills off a lot of plants and the land animals starve.

Heating the oceans shuts down the currents that circulate dissolved oxygen. The sea creatures can't breathe. Nine-tenths of sea life and two-thirds of land life dies out and slimy microbes rule the wasted world. It's almost the end of Earth – but not quite. A few animals hang on. After a million years the planet cools and new life forms emerge.

What happened long ago makes our present problems look like a pixie's picnic party. But it could be a warning – after all, scientists think we're heading for 6°C of warming too. Or are we? This time we've got something to help us. I'm talking about brains. There's no doubt we're smarter than a giant fish and brighter than a chunky reptile.

Of course our intelligence created the Mighty Planet-Munching Machine and got us into this mess. But we've got the brain-power to know when things are going wrong. And hopefully we possess the wisdom to find a way out.

# WASTED WORLD

# QUIZ

Now find out if you're a
**Wasted World** expert!

# Fearsome fuels

*Our planet is under attack because we're all greedy guzzlers of fuel. Every time we switch on a light, boil an egg or drive a car, we use up fossil fuels that can't be replaced when they run out. Take this quiz and figure out the fearful facts about fuels.*

**1** What strange substances are fragile fossil fuels made from?
**a)** The rotting remains of prehistoric plants and animals
**b)** A natural form of treacle
**c)** Animal poo and garden compost

**2** Which dangerously depleted fossil fuel is likely to run out within the next 50 years?
**a)** Your big sister's old copies of *OK!* magazine
**b)** Coal
**c)** Oil

**3** What ghastly greenhouse gas is belched into the air every time your mum or dad drives you to school?
**a)** Methane
**b)** Bad breath
**c)** Carbon dioxide

**4** When coal is burnt it releases awesome energy that we use every day, but how much of the energy generated actually reaches us as electricity?
**a)** All of it
**b)** One-third of it
**c)** Less than five per cent

**5** What are fantastic farmers in Brazil using to make the brilliant biofuel ethanol?
**a)** Sugar cane
**b)** Candy floss
**c)** Tree sap

**6** Why are many scientists against using nuclear power as a source of energy?
**a)** They haven't figured out how to harness its energy yet.
**b)** They haven't figured out how to deal safely with the radioactive waste.
**c)** They're worried the heat will melt the planet.

**7** What is the name given to oil when it is first taken from the ground, before it's refined into all its useful products?
**a)** Crude oil
**b)** Rude oil
**c)** Raw oil

**8** What is the most common form of awesome renewable energy used worldwide?
**a)** Nuclear power
**b)** Solar power
**c)** Wind power

**Answers:**
1a; 2c; 3c; 4b; 5a; 6b; 7a; 8c

## Radical renewable energy

*You might think the
best way to save the
world is simply to
catch evil Professor
Z and put paid to his
painful plans, but for
many years scientists
have been looking at
other ways of saving
the world. Most
of them agree that
renewable resources
are the way forward.*

*Use the clues below to unravel the renewable
solution and save the world.*

**1** WARM FIND (2 words)
CLUE: This breezy place can turn air into energy.

**2** WEAPON CURLER (2 words)
CLUE: This explosive energy could be the fuel of the
future.

**3** PEARL SALON (2 words)
CLUE: This super sunshine collector is a bright idea.

**4** BOIL FUSE (1 word)
CLUE: Plant petrol perhaps?

**5** COACHED MILE TERRY (2 words)
CLUE: A wall to hold back water until its rushing energy is required.

**6** GAMER HOTEL (1 word)
CLUE: This type of energy belches its way up from underneath the Earth.

**7** LEOPARD WIT (2 words)
CLUE: This watery energy uses the magic of the moon.

**8** PEAR WE VOW (2 words)
CLUE: Energy sourced from the surface of the sea.

**Answers:**
**1** WIND FARM
**2** NUCLEAR POWER
**3** SOLAR PANEL
**4** BIOFUELS
**5** HYDROELECTRIC DAM
**6** GEOTHERMAL
**7** TIDAL POWER
**8** WAVE POWER

## Amazing Earth-saving inventions

*People have come up with all sorts of potty plans to save our warming world. Can you work out which of these are genuine ideas and which are just a load of old planet-polluting rubbish.*

**1** A Swedish inventor dreamt up a "flower" lamp that monitors energy use. When you're being energy efficient, the metal petals unfold to say congrats – it's a blooming ingenious idea!

**2** In the late twentieth century, scientists in America invented an energy-efficient car that was powered purely by methane captured from cow farts.

**3** Since the nineteenth century, scientists have been working on a special cell that can capture the energy from sunlight and turn it into electricity.

**4** An insane inventor in Switzerland has designed a giant glass dome that can be constructed over cities to stop ghastly greenhouse gases escaping into the atmosphere.

**5** In some countries, the gas given off by decay at landfill sites is being harnessed and used to generate electricity.

**6** "Living roofs" are the latest way of making buildings greener. Covering your roof with moss – and even growing flowers there – can improve insulation and filter pollutants out of rainwater.

**7** A group of German geniuses have developed a green way of getting about – special springy stilts that you strap to your legs to allow you to take great leaps forwards (and upwards).

**8** A group of companies have got together to create a pollution-free plane that can travel long distances powered only by the wind and air currents.

**Answers:**
**1** TRUE. The imaginative inventors wanted to raise people's awareness of energy use in their homes.
**2** FALSE. There have been many great ideas for green cars, but cow fart-fuelled vehicle isn't one of them!
**3** TRUE. And they succeeded – solar cells are used in all sorts of gadgets all over the world. There are even "solar farms" that provide green electricity for hundreds of homes.
**4** FALSE. Everyone would be sweltering in the ginormous greenhouse – and just how would you build one big enough anyway?
**5** TRUE. Super scientists figured that if we must get rid of our garbage in landfill, we might as well make the most of the gruesome gas it gives off.
**6** TRUE. Green gardens on the roofs of buildings have lots of environmental benefits.
**7** TRUE. There's already a craze for this cool gadget in Germany. It's a good form of exercise and great for the environment, too.
**8** FALSE. They might be working on less gas-guzzling plane engines, but gliding on the air wouldn't get you very far.

# Weird weather

*Remember all that whacky weather we looked at, caused by horrible human activity and ghastly global warming? Look at the fatal forecasts below and match up the cause with the wild weather effect.*

**Causes:**

**1** Overheated air caused by global warming sucks all the moisture out of plants and soil and dries up the land. If no rain falls for a long time, the deathly dryness is known as _____.

**2** One eerie effect of global warming is that our oceans are hotting up. Scientists think this accounts for the increase in the power of _____.

**3** As horrible humans cut down trees and drain marshlands to make room for settlements, the Earth's natural sponges get smaller, which can result in _____.

**4** A fantastic phenomenon known as _____ is made worse by global warming and can cause wild weather all over the world.

**5** Hot air gets hotter as gruesome global warming occurs, and can cause lo-o-ong periods of horribly hot weather known as _____.

**6** Chopping down trees, overgrazing and overuse of land for farming have all contributed to a deathly drying-out of the Earth called _____.

**7** In Greenland and Antarctica _____ caused by our warming world could result in fatal flooding.

IT'S A CHILLING PROSPECT!

**8** Under the eye of a storm, swirling seas bulge and race to shore. These wrecking waves are known as _____.

**Effects:**
**a)** Hurricanes
**b)** Heatwaves
**c)** Desertification
**d)** El Niño
**e)** Melting ice caps
**f)** Storm surges
**g)** Drought
**h)** Floods

# Poisonous pollution

*Every year, half-witted humans chuck away millions of tonnes of rubbish, release poisonous chemicals into rivers and seas, and burp out toxic waste into the air from cars and factories. How clued up are you about the dangers of poisonous pollution?*

**1** What type of putrid pollution results when coal smoke mixes with water vapour in the air? (CLUE: It's a dangerous downpour)

**2** Which killer water-polluting chemical can bung up your brain and make you mad? (CLUE: You wouldn't want to gulp down this murderous metal)

**3** Plastic bags in the sea cause confusion for creatures fishing for food. What do they mistake the polluting plastic for? (CLUE: I wonder if they enjoy them with ice cream)

**4** What fatal farming substances are putting poisons in the ground, killing creatures and infecting water supplies? (CLUE: It's a right pest)

**5** Which protective layer of the Earth's atmosphere is being destroyed by killer chemicals known as CFCs? (CLUE: O – this area's a hole heap of trouble)

**6** Which polluting product made from oil comes in more than 50 types, almost none of which can be recycled? (CLUE: Everything from polystyrene to plumbing pipes)

**7** What kind of wicked waste remains deadly for hundreds of thousands of years after it's thrown away? (CLUE: Radioactive rubbish)

**8** What sticky substance can leak from pipelines and spill from ships to pollute ground and water and laying waste to wildlife? (CLUE: Some may say it's a crude catastrophe)

**Answers:**
1 Acid rain
2 Mercury
3 Jellyfish
4 Pesticides
5 Ozone
6 Plastic
7 Nuclear
8 Oil

# HORRIBLE INDEX

**142**

radioactive waste 21–2, 26, 113
rainforests 15–17, 79, 105, 114
rats 101
raw materials 12–13
reusing things 25, 73
recycling things 9, 24, 115, 118–19
refineries 26, 38
renewable energy 112
rich countries 28, 51–2, 54
rubbish/rubbish dumps 22, 25, 44, 47, 52, 79, 118–19

sea levels, rising 84, 93–5, 97, 103–5, 111
seabirds 19
seas 18, 21, 25, 46, 50, 55, 65, 72–3, 82, 84, 86, 90, 94–5, 103, 105, 127
sewage 79–80
shampoo 41
sheep 74
shower gel 41
silver, supplies of 14
skeletons 29, 66
sludge 26
smog (smoky fog) 37
soil 17, 21, 33, 54, 60, 69–73, 78, 117
solar panels 116, 118
sorghum (food crop) 74
storms 56, 75–84, 97
sulphur/sulphides 26, 49, 62
summer 52, 61, 63, 88, 100
sunburn 64
supermarkets 52–4, 119
swamps, swamped 95
sweat 57–9, 61
swordfish 18

teak (rainforest hardwood) 17
televisions 14, 123
Teller, Edward (American scientist) 109
temperature 58–60, 103–4, 117, 124, 127

thermostats 56, 124
tornadoes 84
toxic waste 21–2, 25–9, 31–3, 44, 79, 91–2, 110, 125
trash 6, 21–33
travel/transport 9, 42, 44, 52–4, 115, 118
trees 9–10, 17, 23, 33, 35, 38, 46, 66, 73–4, 77, 99, 113, 122
troposphere (atmospheric layer) 87
tuna 18
turbines, making electricity 35, 118
turtles 25
typhoons 82, 84, 95
tyres 33

ultraviolet (invisible rays) 49
uranium 113

vapour trails 52
vegetables 53–4, 118
vicious circles 104–6
volcanoes, violent 50, 127

waste 6, 21–2, 25–9, 31–3, 44, 79, 91–2, 125
water/water vapour 7–9, 19, 30–1, 38, 41, 50, 55, 64, 69–70, 72–9, 81–2, 85, 88–9, 91–4, 96, 104–5, 108–9, 112, 124
weather, wild 5, 43–4, 56, 60, 63, 69–70, 87, 97, 102–3, 112
weeds, killers of 26
wheat (food crop) 70–1
winds 45, 56, 64, 69–71, 81, 83, 87, 112, 118
winter 52, 63, 100–1, 104
wood 35–6, 43
work 34, 52
Wragge, Clement (British scientist) 72, 83

zinc (steel-making mineral) 14